PRAISE FOR NAKKIAH LUI

"I've been in awe of Nakkiah since I saw her play *This Heaven* at Belvoir in 2013. I can't remember a time before seeing this play where I had seen Aboriginal people represented in the present day. Quite often the plays I had performed in or watched had been retrospective, and *This Heaven* spoke to me as a modern Black woman. I felt seen, I felt understood. Her work continues to explore what Aboriginality is in all its dimensions. My sister is brave, because you can always tell that she has spilled her heart onto the page. She is also insanely good at comedy, and uses that to challenge the privileges that colonisation continues to give non-Aboriginal Australians. She punches up by giving nuance and humanity back to her community. I loved playing Rose in *Black is the New White* not only because of all the great lines she gifted me, but also having the opportunity to perform with so many talented performers of colour. There were no egos on this project because everyone loved what they were a part of. I hope that audiences who see her work take whatever the play made them feel and do something to even the playing field for Aboriginal and Torres Strait Islander people. Her work makes me believe that art can change the world." **Miranda Tapsell**

"Sneakily disguised as a whacky Christmas rom-com comes this shrewd remoulding of the national chat about race in contemporary Australia. It's as if Nakkiah shows us our conversational display home, full of all those recliner rockers we've always retreated to in our discussions of race identity, and begins carefully rearranging them, and then picks them up and hurls them about the stage with savage glee. What a thrilling new voice in Australian theatre." **Richard Roxburgh**

"Her writing, whether devastating or hilarious, has always shown a great deal of accessible humanity and relentless intelligence." ***The Guardian***

"We needed a new David Williamson, someone who speaks to Australia and Australians now. We've found her in Nakkiah." **Alex Broun**

"If there is such a thing as a rockstar playwright, Nakkiah Lui is it." **Fran Kelly, ABC Radio National**

NAKKIAH LUI

BLACK IS THE NEW WHITE

First published in 2019

Allen & Unwin
83 Alexander Street
Crows Nest NSW 2065
Australia
Phone: (61 2) 8425 0100
Email: info@allenandunwin.com
Web: www.allenandunwin.com

A catalogue record for this book is available from the National Library of Australia

ISBN 978 1 76052 734 1

Internal design by Bookhouse, Sydney
Set in 12/16 pt Adobe Garamond Pro by Bookhouse, Sydney
Printed and bound in Australia by Pegasus Media & Logistics
10

The paper in this book is FSC® certified. FSC® promotes environmentally responsible, socially beneficial and economically viable management of the world's forests.

For Joan.
For Jenny.
For Jack.
For Lowie.
For Keesh.
And most of all, for my silver lining of colonisation, Gabe.

CONTENTS

FOREWORD

I love Christmas. My family love Christmas. I have never missed a Christmas with my family. That would be akin to some kind of sacrilege. I love the excitement you get from putting up the tree, singing along to Christmas carols that you only know two lines of. I love wrapping presents and trying to curl the ribbon just right. I love shopping with my family in the overcrowded shopping centres with their too-cold air conditioning and getting a kebab from the food court. I love the smells of cooking all day and getting dressed up to not leave the house. I love watching Christmas movies from the northern hemisphere that are filled with snow and cosiness, whilst I sweat it out in front of a fan. I love being with my family. A family that is changing as we get older, new members and additions joining each year and sometimes, sadly, a loved one leaving.

But Christmas isn't where the play started. That's where the play ended up. *Black is the New White* started as two separate conversations. The first was about love. I was having a conversation with a cousin of mine who is this fabulous young Aboriginal woman, a gorgeous and great mum, a lover of Instagram and lycra and the hashtag #yummymummy. We were talking politics (talking politics is like talking sports in my family) and for some reason love came up, and she said that communities should try to stick together, to "get bigger and better and Blacker" . . . her racial/political beliefs could be seen as akin to Black separatism and I didn't necessarily agree with her (I had dated one Aboriginal person and not had much luck—they turned out to be a cousin).

However, at the same time, both my parents are Aboriginal, same as hers, so why did she hold those beliefs and why didn't I? I thought it was a really interesting conversation to be having with someone who, I would say, is part of this new emerging Aboriginal middle class. It was around this time that I looked at the census and discovered a surprising statistic: 74 per cent of Aboriginal people who get married marry non-Aboriginal people. We were the community most likely to marry a race outside of our own. I found this really interesting . . . it intrigued me as to who this 74 per cent are.

Primarily because I was one of them. I fell in love as I started writing this play. I'd got engaged by the time it had finished. To a White man. I was part of this 74 per cent . . . but that really bothered me, because, to me, my love was way more than a statistic. But there it was . . . an overwhelming statistic that was vastly different to the trends of non-aboriginal Australians.

That led me to investigate how my own family had shifted over the last two generations, and how this had affected their definition of class. I was really interested in how we identify ourselves in terms of our racial and cultural backgrounds, and how that intersects with class. What does it mean to be successful? Especially as Aboriginal people, when you come from a community that is so often politicised.

I also wanted to present a family of Aboriginal people that hasn't been seen before, not just on stage, I would say, but within the canon of Australian artistic works. That is, an Aboriginal family who have money, who are not necessarily oppressed, but are culturally quite strong. So I had the idea of putting forth that family, because, for me, that was similar to what I've grown up with.

The way my family has celebrated Christmas has changed over the years: from cold meat platters at my nana's tiny little fibro house we all crammed into before running under the sprinkler; big picnics with extended family in the local park as the kids ran around in what were called "the piddle pools"; then later, to hot meals with gourmet cuts of meat, caviar and Bellinis in the morning, swims in the pool in the afternoon; then, a "white Christmas" on the other side of the equator one year, together and loving Christmas in a foreign but familiar land.

But all still the same in the end—with your family, bickering and happy. The evolution of my family Christmas celebrations seemed to reflect a much bigger discussion I was trying to figure out: what is it to be Aboriginal and middle class? Is that even a thing?

That journey to middle class was fought for. The ability to have hope and love and celebration, in my heart, is because my parents, my grandparents and ancestors fought incredibly hard against all the odds to make sure the ones who came after them would have a good life.

And if being Aboriginal and middle class is a thing, if that's what has happened in my family, what does it mean to have that privilege? What does it mean to be an Aboriginal person with power?

Over the last ten years I've watched my parents transform into serious foodies. Just watching that happen made me want to present a family of Aboriginals drinking on stage in a way that wasn't politicised. That in and of itself then becomes a statement. I wanted to say, "Here's a family who are like you." I wanted to write something that didn't come from a place of sorrow, or from death, or from oppression, where I'd have to rehash that intergenerational trauma. This was actually about something that had hope and happiness in it.

For me, having privilege gives you the power to be seen as a human and not just a racial identity. If I, as a kinda-middle-class Aboriginal person, could put an Aboriginal family on stage and have them be seen as people, individuals, and not just Aboriginal, if I could get the people in the audience to look at that family and say "they're just like me", then maybe that would be my way of creating hope for others.

I wrote this play as I fell in love and my life changed around me, consequently changing my family's life as well (they love their White son). My own little love story hit all the rom-com tropes: it had the "meet cute" (the serendipitous meeting of the two "destined to fall in love", the more unusual the better), the over-the-top romantic gestures (think John Cusack standing with a boom box outside the bedroom window), it even had the coordinated dance sequence. I wanted to write something that made me as happy as my life was. I love romantic comedies. I love falling in love with characters. I love the feeling of elation that you get when you really love a story; I call it the "Tingles". I wanted to write a play that gives you the tingles, that makes you want to laugh and dance and leaves you with those tingles as you walk out of the theatre and into your life.

My beautiful grandmother, Joan, always used to say to me, "what can you do if you can't laugh?" I say this to myself every day. I think laughter is the heart opening the door, and the more we can laugh, the more open and bigger our hearts get.

Nakkiah Lui
November 2018

DRAMATIS PERSONAE

Charlotte Gibson – mid to late 20s

Francis Smith – mid to late 20s

Ray Gibson – mid 50s to early 60s, constantly wearing a virtual reality headset

Joan Gibson – mid 50s to early 60s

Rose Jones – late 20s to early 30s

Sonny Jones – late 20s to early 30s

Dennison Smith – mid 50s to early 60s

Marie Smith – mid 50s to early 60s

NOTES

SETTING

Sprawling expensive holiday home owned by the Gibsons, located in the bush on ancestral land.

OVERLAPPING

A slash (/) in a character's line denotes where the *following character's line* should begin.

A slash (/) at the beginning of a line denotes a *complete* overlap with the *following character's line.*

An ellipsis (. . .) indicates a pause/silence.

THE PLAY

Genre: Think a Christmas play, a rom-com, and a homage to the family dramas of Australia's past.

I listened to *Right Back Where We Started From* by Maxine Nightingale a lot while writing this.

SCENE 1

CHRISTMAS EVE

Lounge room and dining room adjoined in open space living. The walls are artfully adorned with family photos in expensive frames. Wrapped presents sit around the room and the remains of present wrapping paraphernalia lay around the room. Cicadas buzz. FRANCIS *plays a modern, experimental classical piece on the cello.*

NARRATOR

Many people know the name Ray Gibson, but what they don't know is that Ray Gibson was the son of a drover. As a young boy he moved around often, and his world was safe and insular. As a teen he moved to the big smoke and all of a sudden he felt like an outsider, like he couldn't find his place.

This turned him into a fighter, both on the streets and in the ring. He would train in the mornings, doing speed and punching exercises, and then use what he learnt at training in the evenings: getting into punch ups and running from the coppers.

Ray Gibson was an unhappy young man. One day Ray's mum dragged him to church. It was at church that a nice White lady gave Ray a book. It was called *Where Do We Go From Here: Chaos or Community?* by Martin Luther King. This book made Ray Gibson feel like he wasn't alone in the world.

To Ray, the book was about hope: how the one thing mankind has *is* hope and it was with hope that he went forward. Inspired by the words of Dr King, Ray Gibson went forward and never turned back.

The man you are watching is not Ray Gibson. Of course it's not. Ray is Aboriginal. This is Francis Smith. He's White. He is also the fiancé of Charlotte, Ray's youngest daughter. But you see, Ray does not know this yet. In fact, no one knows this yet. But that is about to change very soon.

Oh! And who am I? Some people call me The Narrator, but I prefer: the Spirit of Christmas.

CHARLOTTE *enters, balancing a laptop in one hand and a glass of water in the other, headphones in and having a Skype meeting.*

CHARLOTTE Yes, but that isn't anyone's prerogative aside from his – I said that's not anyone's prero . . . prerogative. Prerogative. Yes. That is a word. Pardon? That's what I've been saying.

Yes, but you're just saying what I said a different way.

I would be very happy to have a conversation with the minister about those changes. Of course. Why wouldn't I be? I mean, I've had the same conversation with all of his predecessors and his advisers, and their predecessors and their advisers . . . why not the man himself? Yes. Thanks. You too. Merry Christmas.

FRANCIS *stops playing. He pours* CHARLOTTE *a glass of wine. She hesitates, and then takes it.*

CHARLOTTE Do you ever just hate your job?

FRANCIS No, I love my job.

CHARLOTTE You play the cello, of course you love your job.

Maybe hate is too strong a word. Maybe I mean dislike.

Dislike. I dislike my job. No, I definitely mean hate.

I hate my job.

Franny, I hate my job.

FRANCIS Darling, I hate when you call me Franny.

CHARLOTTE Franny, maybe I should just give up practising law to work in a shop?

FRANCIS I don't know . . . I think it'd be pretty shit.

CHARLOTTE Here, do me a favour and pass me the paper. Not that paper, the other one. The gold one. And the scissors. And the tape. Thank you, my darling.

FRANCIS Who's the blow-up pink flamingo for?

CHARLOTTE Mum. Last year I got her a gold swan and she hated it. So this year, a pink flamingo.

FRANCIS How passive aggressive of you.

CHARLOTTE It's not like that. We're not White people. *It's just a joke.* Also, you got her this.

CHARLOTTE *hands* FRANCIS *a box.*

FRANCIS Gypsy Water? What kind of name is Gypsy Water?

CHARLOTTE She loves it. They only stock it in Sweden. After I casually mentioned that she had run out, you went online and ordered it for her especially.

FRANCIS I did?

CHARLOTTE Yes.

FRANCIS Isn't Gypsy Water a form of cultural appropriation? Aren't Gypsies actually a cultural group? Weren't you lecturing me about that the other day? I believe the precise words were: "All inequalities are connected and privilege is thinking something isn't an issue because it's not an issue to you."

CHARLOTTE . . . Yes. And my point that cultural appropriation is cultural colonisation still stands BUT this smells so good.

And I think it's a reference to some culture thing . . . of the makers . . . of the people . . . who make the scent . . . the perfume scent.

FRANCIS They have Gypsies in Sweden?

CHARLOTTE There are gypsies everywhere.

FRANCIS You say that there's one living under the stairs.

And am I giving the Gypsy perfume to this woman here?

FRANCIS *motions to a picture on the wall.*

CHARLOTTE Yes.

FRANCIS Now I see where you get your looks from.

CHARLOTTE Did you really just say that?

FRANCIS I did.

CHARLOTTE Disgusting. Kiss me.

They kiss. CHARLOTTE *dawdles over to get a chocolate from a box across the room and dawdles back.* FRANCIS *continues to look at the pictures.*

CHARLOTTE Mum was beautiful. I mean, it's not like she isn't now. She is, great for her age, you'll see.

Why do we say "for their age"?

That's so ageist. And sexist. Because we really only say it for women, don't we?

God, all these behaviours are just so ingrained in me. It's disgusting. I'm disgusting.

Anyways.

That was her at her . . . her grad ball for nursing, I think.

CHARLOTTE *continues to wrap presents.*

FRANCIS Is this your dad and Bill Clinton?

CHARLOTTE Oh yeah, they're buddies.

FRANCIS Ha. Buddies. You say that so casually.

CHARLOTTE We call him Uncle.

FRANCIS Really?

CHARLOTTE Of course not. I was joking. We barely know the bloke. But please remember to try and sound as impressed as you just did when you meet my father. It'll appeal to his ego. His huge ego.

FRANCIS I won't have to try.

CHARLOTTE Aren't you used to this stuff?

FRANCIS My father was never as popular with the proletariat as your father was. Or popular with anyone actually.

CHARLOTTE I bet they both just felt a chill run up their spines.

FRANCIS Well, let's just say we don't have pictures of my dad and Bill Clinton around the house. Look at them. Bill and Ray. Ray and Bill. A real pair of lady killers.

CHARLOTTE If you really want to be entertained ask Dad if he thinks Bill Clinton did it. He'll rant for hours.

FRANCIS He thinks Bill did or didn't?

CHARLOTTE Thinks he didn't. Thinks that he was set up by "The System."

But when I ask him why "The System" would want to bring down a powerful, rich, White man, he can never give me an answer.

FRANCIS Regardless, that doesn't mean that he didn't . . . receive anything /

CHARLOTTE / Just say it, Francis. Get head. Yes, you're right.

But by this time, Dad has usually had another few wines and it's time to get a cheeseboard and then watch *The Shawshank Redemption* for the one millionth time.

FRANCIS So your Dad likes *The Shawshank Redemption, Forrest Gump, Braveheart, The Godfather, Wanted* /

CHARLOTTE / *Not Wanted*, *Taken*. Or really anything with Liam Neeson. But in particular *Taken*.

FRANCIS The one about the guy who saves his daughter from the sex trade?

CHARLOTTE Yep.

I think he secretly wishes my sister and I would get into some situation he could rescue us from.

FRANCIS So, *The Shawshank Redemption*, *Forrest Gump*, *Braveheart*, *The Godfather* and *Taken*.

For a Black man your dad sure has White taste in movies.

CHARLOTTE He's got White taste in a lot of things.

FRANCIS Like exquisitely designed holiday homes?

CHARLOTTE'S *phone rings. She ignores it.*

FRANCIS Who are you ignoring?

CHARLOTTE Pennelope, the producer who wants me to host that new current affairs show.

FRANCIS Just tell her you're moving to New York. Just say: "Sorry, I am moving to New York with my debonair and dashing White fiancé to follow our dreams and I have no time for your pithy TV show."

CHARLOTTE Tell her just like that?

FRANCIS Just like that.

CHARLOTTE'S *phone beeps. She plays a voicemail.*

PRODUCER *Charlotte, darling. It's Pennelope. From The Studio. I don't mean to be stalking you but – OKAY – You got me – I AM stalking you. Everyone is so keen to have you on and we'd be wanting to announce after New Year. Make a real landmark thing. Because that's what it is – a landmark thing. Not to put on the pressure – but please tell me how else I can put the pressure on. Love you, love your work, get back to me. Oh, also we absolutely loved the video of your father. It's the Martin Luther King moment for Australia.*

CHARLOTTE Ugh. My father is not the Martin Luther King of Australia.

He is so far from Martin Luther King. If only people knew.

Martin Luther King had a dream and my father is a total nightmare.

Maybe I won't do anything. I won't do the show, I'll quit law. I'll even turn down the scholarship in New York.

FRANCIS And what are you going to do instead of having adventures with me in New York, sweet poppet?

CHARLOTTE Sweet poppet? That's a new one.

FRANCIS Thought I'd try it. Like it?

CHARLOTTE Not really.

Maybe I'll stay in Sydney and work at that artisanal bread shop.

FRANCIS "Artisanal bread shop" is the worst phrase I've ever heard any human being say.

CHARLOTTE But imagine not having to bring your work home with you.

FRANCIS I think you're being a bit classist and romanticising the poor and the working class.

CHARLOTTE Okay, I am not being classist or romanticising the poor or the working class.

FRANCIS You're not?

CHARLOTTE Okay, well, first of all, aren't you being classist assuming it's only poor or working-class people who work in shops? Maybe there are rich people working in shops? Also, as a Black woman /

FRANCIS / Here we go.

CHARLOTTE As a Black woman, a White man, such as yourself, should not be discrediting the place of privilege from which you make your judgement, Francis. Which, may I point out, is the Whitest name possible, Francis.

FRANCIS Well, look, it's not my fault that my name is Francis. It's not my fault I was born White /

CHARLOTTE / Here we go again.

FRANCIS More wine?

FRANCIS *kisses* CHARLOTTE *to shut her up.*

CHARLOTTE Did you kiss me to shut me up?

FRANCIS Yes. See, us White people have all the solutions. Just think, soon it will just be me and you in /

CHARLOTTE / In New York.

FRANCIS In New York.

They kiss again.

FRANCIS What if you did quit? You'd quit and do what?

CHARLOTTE I don't know. Not think. Do some painting. Make babies. Little bi-racial babies.

FRANCIS Ambitious.

CHARLOTTE It is. One could argue I'm changing the world by eradicating racism through procreation.

FRANCIS By staying at home and making lots of babies?

CHARLOTTE Yes.

FRANCIS So freeloading?

CHARLOTTE Precisely.

FRANCIS I'm pretty sure we can only have one of those in this relationship.

CHARLOTTE You're not a freeloader.

FRANCIS Yes, I am.

CHARLOTTE Do you really think that?

FRANCIS Well, it's not so much a thought as a fact. I'm a detriment.

CHARLOTTE Have you been speaking to your father again?

FRANCIS No.

CHARLOTTE Don't lie.

FRANCIS Look, it's not as if he's wrong.

CHARLOTTE He's wrong. You are not a detriment.

FRANCIS That is not what you usually say about my race.

CHARLOTTE Okay, yes, you may be White, and from the people who stole my family's land and tried to kill us. Yes! You may be all of those things but you are not / a

FRANCIS My father hates me and your father will most likely hate me because I can't look after his little girl. And I'm a gubbo.

CHARLOTTE It's *gubba*.

FRANCIS Charlotte, how much is the perfume I'm meant to be giving your mother?

CHARLOTTE Don't worry about it.

FRANCIS How much is don't worry about it?

CHARLOTTE Seriously, Francis.

FRANCIS How much is it, Charlotte?

CHARLOTTE Really, Francis, come on . . . this is so gauche . . .

FRANCIS I don't know if you're using that ironically or not.

CHARLOTTE Stop making me sound like this person. This . . . uppity . . . weird about money person.

FRANCIS Well, tell me how much it is.

CHARLOTTE $450.

FRANCIS $450! Charlotte, that's more than my weekly allowance!

Your parents will think that I can afford that type of thing. That type of lifestyle.

And that would be a lie.

CHARLOTTE I don't care what they think about you. Well, I care what they think about you.

But I mean, I don't care how they value your finances. I just wanted to give Mum something she liked. And . . . she is going to like you . . . but . . . Look, I wanted to get her on side because when my father . . .

When my father finds out about the engagement . . . Well . . . he might make it hard . . .

Please don't be mad.

FRANCIS Charlotte, just as long as you realise that I'm poor.

CHARLOTTE Oh, I totally realise that.

FRANCIS I'm very poor. This poor artist act isn't an act.

CHARLOTTE Well, at least till your parents die.

FRANCIS They'll most likely cut me out of the will.

CHARLOTTE Francis, I was joking. They're rich, White people. They'll probably never die.

FRANCIS God, Charlotte, don't tempt fate.

CHARLOTTE None of that matters to me. Your family. Your money. Your weird feet.

FRANCIS Look, don't speak to me from your place of normal foot privilege—

CHARLOTTE You matter to me. This man. This man here in front of me. Under these useless rags you call clothes.

CHARLOTTE *starts undressing* FRANCIS.

CHARLOTTE Under this useless shirt. Under these useless, useless pants. Under these especially useless underpants. The original tool of White oppression. Underpants. Under all this is the man I love. Just a man.

FRANCIS I love you too.

CHARLOTTE My darling, to me, you are the silver lining of colonisation.

They start to get it on.

SCENE 2

Lounge room. JOAN *and* RAY *enter.* JOAN *struggling to hold numerous presents and bags.* RAY *tapping away at his phone.* JOAN *drops everything.*

JOAN Ray! Get off your phone!

RAY Wait there . . .

Get this – old mate sack-a-whack Dennison Smith just tweeted that rocket is better than iceberg. What a tosser! Just when you think the man can't be any more of an idiot, turns out he's even stupid when it comes to lettuce.

JOAN Get off your bloody phone and help with the bags.

RAY Alright, alright. But first, what should I say to him? "Lettuce pray for tossers like you." Hmm. No good. Joan, what should I reply? Joan?

JOAN You know, I hadn't wanted a cigarette for a good twenty years until you joined Twitter. Now I want one every day.

RAY What's a good reply? Joan, what should I say?

JOAN Tell him that "Iceberg brought the *Titanic* down" or something. I really don't care.

RAY Yes, that's it! Brilliant. *"Iceberg brought the* Titanic *down. Who is king of the lettuce now? NOT rocket. Sucker."*

JOAN Give that here. Now go get the rest of the bags.

RAY *leaves and brings in more bags.* JOAN *starts unpacking presents.*

NARRATOR

Joan met Ray at a Deaths in Custody March in 1980 in Redfern, Sydney. It was love at first sight. She had just returned from working on Thursday Island as a remote area nurse. She loved it there: the soft harshness of isolated island life, the sea water and the sun.

She was from the heart of the bush and grew up in a tent by the river. But by the sea she felt at home. And up on the islands, as a RAN, she had a lot of responsibility. She helped people. People trusted her. And she trusted them.

Joan had many lovers before meeting Ray. He doesn't know that. Before deciding to leave Torres Strait, she was almost going to marry a young Swedish doctor. He had the bluest eyes she had ever seen and sometimes he even modelled.

Joan thought about him often. Like she is now. Not wondering what could have been but just of his blue eyes and what a fine shade of blue they were.

RAY *drags the last of the bags in.*

JOAN The sky always looks so blue out here, doesn't it?

RAY Did we bring my golf clubs? Did – what's her name – the little Asian lady – your mate – did she pack my clubs?

JOAN Her name's Beth, Ray. And no, you have a new set here. The ones I got you last Christmas.

RAY But that doesn't have my lucky club.

JOAN You have a lucky club?

RAY Yes, I do. It's the driver I used to hit the eagle.

JOAN I don't know what any of that means / but

RAY / It's a type of / club

JOAN / You'll be fine, Ray.

RAY Well, I suppose I'll have to be. You know, you could have asked if I wanted to bring my clubs.

JOAN And you could have packed your own bags.

RAY When was the gardener last here? Looks like the lawn hasn't been done in a while.

JOAN His mother has been ill, so he went home to spend Christmas with her.

RAY Well, I guess I'll have to mow the place myself now.

JOAN It'll be good for / you

RAY / He just tweeted! Dennison. He said: "They don't call it rocket science for nothing." But he didn't tweet it at me. But I know it's about me. It's totally about me. Didn't even have the balls to tweet it to my face! That piece of /

JOAN / Ray. Stop it. It's just lettuce.

RAY It's not just lettuce. It's that he's wrong.

JOAN Says who?

RAY Says the world. It's just the way it is. It's the natural order of things. It's truth, and you can't run around saying that something true isn't true.

JOAN Who cares?

RAY I care, Joan, I care. If we can't stand for the truth of the simple things in life then what can we stand for?

JOAN I want a cigarette.

RAY You know, Joan, if you were to start I wouldn't mind. I always thought you were very sexy when you smoked.

JOAN Did you now?

RAY Yes.

JOAN When I used to huff on a cigarette like this?

RAY Yes.

JOAN And how about like this?

RAY Yes.

JOAN And like this?

JOAN *starts coughing ferociously.*

RAY No – definitely not.

Wait – Joan, are you okay? Joan. Joan!

JOAN That's lung cancer, Ray. And you better find that sexy because that's what I'm going to get if you push me to start smoking because you won't get off that stupid phone.

RAY Hey, look, the channel is repeating my speech tonight!

JOAN I said no phones!

RAY I'm only looking at my phone because this is important! They're showing my speech and interview again tonight.

JOAN Okay.

RAY Back by popular demand!

JOAN That's very nice, Ray.

RAY We should watch it again.

JOAN We've watched it quite a lot . . .

RAY But I mean, we should watch it with the girls.

JOAN But the girls saw it when it went to air.

RAY But we haven't watched it together as a family yet. Not yet. And we should watch it as a family.

JOAN Ray, we've got Charlotte's new boyfriend and his parents coming as well. I don't / think

RAY / It'll be a way to introduce them to the family.

JOAN — Ray, there's probably better ways to introduce them to the family.

RAY — Like what?

JOAN — Like, I don't know . . . Like talking to them. Over dinner. Sharing stories. Getting to know each other's values. You know, just, regular things people do when meeting each other for the first time.

RAY — Well, that's what my speech does. I talk about our family values, do I not?

JOAN — Ray, your speech was about the current state of racial politics in Australia.

RAY — Exactly. Family values.

JOAN — Ray, don't you think it's a little intense to talk about these things straight away?

RAY — You've never thought so before.

JOAN — Charlotte is bringing someone for Christmas. The first man she has brought home in years.

RAY — It's bound to come up.

JOAN Then let it come up naturally. But politics, race, all that. To the side, okay? It's Christmas!

RAY Okay.

JOAN You promise?

RAY Yes, Joan.

JOAN You know, I like it when you're agreeable. It's very sexy.

RAY Do you like it when I'm agreeable like this?

RAY *pulls an agreeable pose.*

JOAN Mmm . . . yes.

RAY Or how about like this?

RAY *pulls a very agreeable pose. They start kissing. They start to undress each other while the narrator speaks.* JOAN *takes more control, until* RAY *is pretty close to nude.*

NARRATOR

Francis met Charlotte three months ago on a night when he was particularly poor and particularly cold in London.

He is no longer cold. Or in London. But he is still very poor. Something that was never an issue for him, until he fell in love with Charlotte.

You see, Francis is an experimental classical composer, which in our day and age there is not too much demand for. It is an antiquated profession. Much like ballet shoe makers, butter churners and playwrights.

(And we'll pause that there. Hey! Hey! Focus. I'm watching you!)

His father urged him to go into something more relevant. By "relevant" he meant a profession that actually made money. "There is no money in experimental classical composing, Francis," his father told him. Francis rebelled and left for Europe.

He last saw his parents over post-show steak frites at the Ivy in London. Later that evening he saw his mother on Tinder. He swiped left, of course. Though, one does wonder, what preferences Francis had set on his Tinder that made his mother Marie come up at all.

Anyways *(or "resume").*

Now, the fact that there is not much money to be made in the world of modern experimental classical composition is something Francis thinks about often.

In fact, he thinks about this right now, as he ventures out nude to get a snack.

FRANCIS *ventures out nude to get a snack. He sees* RAY *(semi-nude) and* JOAN *kissing and screams.* JOAN *spots him and screams.* FRANCIS *screams more.* RAY *screams. It's a festival of hands covering penises and yelling.*

RAY WHO ARE YOU?

FRANCIS *grabs a pillow to cover up his bits.*

FRANCIS I am so sorry! Oh, God! I should have put on pants. I knew I should have put pants on. I just had this feeling, you / know—

RAY / WHO ARE YOU?

CHARLOTTE *comes wandering in wearing a silk dressing robe.*

CHARLOTTE Francis – can you make me one of those goat cheese things – Oh, God. Mum. Dad.

Why are you – oh no – oh, gross.

JOAN Charlotte! My darling girl! Come here!

JOAN *scoops* CHARLOTTE *into a hug while she looks on, mortified.*

CHARLOTTE Please tell me I didn't interrupt anything. Please tell me that. I beg you. Please.

RAY We tell you?! How about you tell us! Under my roof / in my—

JOAN / Oh, Ray, shut up, she's a grown woman. Charlotte! I should have realised you would arrive before us!

RAY Who is this . . . naked White boy?!

CHARLOTTE Dad, this is Francis. My partner, Francis.

FRANCIS *holds out one hand*

RAY Partner? You mean boyfriend.

RAY *doesn't shake his hand, so* JOAN *does.*

CHARLOTTE I mean partner, Dad.

JOAN I would hug you, but let's save that for when you have some clothes on. Ray, shake his hand.

RAY I'm not shaking a naked White boy's hand. It's not right.

JOAN Shake it.

FRANCIS Look, it's fine. Thank you, but it's fine.

RAY It's not fine. It's disrespectful. How dare he be nude . . . and White . . . under my / roof.

JOAN Raymond! Shake his *fucking* hand.

RAY *gives in and shakes* FRANCIS's *hand.*

FRANCIS I promise I'll try and keep the nudity limited to showers.

Unless you don't want me to shower nude. It's up to you. How I shower. Or not.

That's weird.

Uh, well, I'm going to excuse myself now. To uh . . . put on some clothes.

JOAN *admires* FRANCIS's *bum as he walks away.*

JOAN He is very handsome for a Whitefella, isn't he?

CHARLOTTE Very.

RAY *fixes himself a drink.*

JOAN You're drinking.

RAY Scotch.

JOAN I didn't ask, I observed.

RAY I need it.

JOAN It's barely 10 am.

RAY I just saw my daughter and a White . . . you know . . .

CHARLOTTE I'm sorry you had to see that. He's not usually naked. I mean, most of the time he's quite clothed.

JOAN Ignore your father.

RAY Ignore me? I'm not the one who was naked!

JOAN You know what the fair thing would be to do? Swapsies. You've seen his, now show him yours.

RAY I am not showing the White boy my budhoo, Joan!

JOAN I was joking, Ray. Stop taking everything so seriously.

CHARLOTTE I'm really sorry. We didn't think you were arriving so early.

JOAN How long have you been here?

CHARLOTTE A few days.

JOAN And you didn't tell us sooner?

CHARLOTTE I just needed some time to think. That last case was really . . . hard.

RAY That was a great case, daught!

JOAN It was very public. I was worried about you.

CHARLOTTE No, not hard because it was public.

It just felt that maybe . . .

At certain points . . . I was out of my depth.

RAY Rubbish. You're a leader.

CHARLOTTE Oh, Dad, I'm really not.

RAY You won. The agreements with the mining companies will be made. The communities will be paid. You have made a difference, Charlotte. It was a brilliant case, you won and should be very proud.

CHARLOTTE I mean, from the outside it looks that way.

RAY This was the kind of thing I dreamt about when I was working.

JOAN You mean *we* dreamt about when we were *both* working.

JOAN'S *phone rings.*

JOAN That'll be your sister. I better take it. So good to see my baby again.

JOAN *gives* CHARLOTTE *a kiss and hug and leaves.*

RAY Drink?

CHARLOTTE Bit early, don't you reckon?

RAY It's always 12 o'clock somewhere.

CHARLOTTE Then yes. A big yes.

RAY Is it really always 12 o'clock somewhere?

RAY *fixes* CHARLOTTE *a drink.*

RAY This scotch is 22 years old. Did you know that?

CHARLOTTE No, I did not know that.

RAY See how it's not young and White?
Means it's good.
Makes all the difference.

CHARLOTTE Please don't be hard on him, Dad.

RAY Who?

CHARLOTTE Francis.

RAY The naked White boy?

CHARLOTTE The naked boyfriend. My naked partner.

RAY If he's a decent bloke I won't be hard on him.

CHARLOTTE I'm serious about him.

RAY If you were so serious, why did we only hear about him a few weeks ago?

CHARLOTTE It's been fast.

RAY Is this really the time to get serious about anyone, Charlotte? I heard about the job offer.

CHARLOTTE How?

RAY The head of the network told me at golf.

This is huge, Charlotte. You could be the Aboriginal female version of Waleed Aly.

This could help massively if you ever decide to go into politics.

CHARLOTTE I told you I'm never going into politics.

RAY Yes, but you can be political without going into politics. Look, I've been watching that *House of Cards* show, and these days you probably have more power in politics without going into politics. That's why I joined Twitter.

CHARLOTTE Dad, about Twitter, you really need to stop fighting with people.

RAY No way. They love me fighting with people. I speak the truth. More people probably listen to me now on Twitter than they ever did in politics. Maybe even more than the prime minister?

After my speech went *viral* people were tweeting that I was Australia's Martin Luther King.

CHARLOTTE Oh, Dad.

RAY In fact, the producers were also saying how great it would be for us to have our own segment. Father and daughter talking politics, race and power. The family business.

CHARLOTTE Dad, I don't think race should be described as the family business. It's a little Third Reich.

RAY Which brings me to this White boy—

CHARLOTTE Francis.

RAY Now, you might like this boy / but

CHARLOTTE Dad /

RAY / Okay, Francis. You might like this Francis, but what does he do?

CHARLOTTE He's a composer.

RAY For music?

CHARLOTTE Yes.

RAY Which symphony or orchestra?

CHARLOTTE Not one in particular. He does his own thing. Experimental classical composition.

RAY Experimental classical comp/osition?

CHARLOTTE Don't be so / judgemental.

RAY Christ / !

CHARLOTTE Dad!

RAY I mean, good for him. It's not very serious or intellectual, but good for him.

CHARLOTTE You know what? I think I'm finished with my drink.

RAY Charlotte. Please, sit down. Hear me out. You have a lot coming up. More cases at work, the TV / show . . .

CHARLOTTE I'm not doing the TV show.

RAY Why wouldn't you?

CHARLOTTE I've been offered a scholarship to do my PhD. At Columbia.

RAY That's . . . that's deadly, daught.

CHARLOTTE I know, right?

RAY What doing? What area of law?

CHARLOTTE Not law, actually. I'm hoping to look into cultural studies and the post-colonial identity.

RAY That is quite the switch.

CHARLOTTE I know it's different from what I've been doing the last few years, but it's really not, in a lot of ways. That last case got me thinking about things, Dad. I mean, yes, in the end we got the mining companies to agree. But I've realised I'm most passionate about changing the archaic conversation around race that we have in this country. Dad, it looked like a win but the amount of time it will take for those communities to see any kind of money is close to never.

The Aboriginal community didn't really win. And how can we change the law if our conversations aren't / changing?

RAY / Well, thank God it's a scholarship, right?

CHARLOTTE Right.

RAY Because you wouldn't want to pay money for that kind of thing.

CHARLOTTE What do you mean?

RAY A bunch of academic cultural theory? They're just whingers and losers who wear weird shirts and don't actually ever do anything. All words, no action.

CHARLOTTE Dad, can you hear yourself?

RAY You could actually change things if you were on television. A young Black woman talking about issues that actually matter.

CHARLOTTE Talking about issues that maybe I have no right to be talking about. That I may not properly understand. In a way that is palatable to people who may not want to hear them.

RAY — Exactly! You are an Aboriginal person with a platform. Do you understand how rare that is? Use it!

CHARLOTTE — But shouldn't we be asking why I have a platform? Why me? Because I'm your daughter?

RAY — If that's the case, don't take that for granted.

CHARLOTTE — Or because I speak well and look acceptable? Because I'm palatable? Shouldn't we be asking why me and not others and what that means?

FRANCIS *walks in, this time dressed.*

FRANCIS — Well, you may not recognise me now that I'm fully clothed but, uh, hello again, I'm Francis, it's nice to meet you, sir.

FRANCIS *holds out his hand, but* CHARLOTTE *and* RAY *ignore him.*

RAY — You're being incredibly spoilt, Charlotte.

JOAN *enters.*

JOAN Rose and Sonny are an hour away. But who knows, that boy drives so fast it could be sooner.

My family will be back together again!

CHARLOTTE *storms out of the room.*

JOAN What's wrong with Charlotte?

RAY I think our daughter has finally hit puberty.

FRANCIS Wait, she told me she was over 18.

JOAN *and* RAY *stare at* FRANCIS.

FRANCIS That was a joke. About consent. You said she just hit puberty and usually that means teenagers. So it would mean that I've been sleeping with a . . . never mind.

JOAN We won't.

RAY I'm going to find my golf clubs.

RAY *angrily leaves.*

JOAN I'm very much looking forward to meeting your parents, Francis.

FRANCIS They're very much looking forward to meeting you, Mrs Gibson.

JOAN Please, call me Joan.

FRANCIS Joan.

JOAN When did you say they were arriving?

FRANCIS Well, they're meant to be here fairly soon. They were actually going to call me this morning.

JOAN And what do they do? Your parents?

FRANCIS *is visibly awkward.*

FRANCIS Uh . . . well, my father . . . he worked in . . . uh . . . governance.

JOAN Oh, what area?

FRANCIS Just finance stuff. I don't really know, you know. Gen Y, all that, too busy looking at our phones.

JOAN And your mother?

FRANCIS / My mother has a passion for . . . philanthropy. You know, that kind of / stuff.

RAY *(Off)* JOAN! I can't find my golf clubs!

JOAN Of course he can't. You better give your mum and dad a call. The property can be a little hard to find.

FRANCIS Will do.

JOAN And don't worry about Ray. He's just a grumpy old man.

RAY *(Off)* Joan! You said they were here!

JOAN Bloody hell, Ray, can you wait one second!

RAY *(Off)* It's been one second!

Joan!

JOAN Francis, please, make yourself at home.

FRANCIS Thank you, Mrs . . . Joan. Will do.

RAY *(Off)* Joan!

JOAN Shut up! I'm coming!

JOAN *leaves.* FRANCIS *sits at his cello and starts to play. His phone rings; he stops playing. He goes to answer it but then decides not to. He starts to play the cello again as it rings out.*

SCENE 3

RAY *walks through the lounge with a virtual reality mask, with golf clubs, phone in his hand, glued to the screen, on his way to play golf.* CHARLOTTE *and* FRANCIS *carry in boxes marked "Christmas tree" and "Xmas decorations".* JOAN *pulls out a cigarette and lights it. She relaxes and enjoys her cigarette.*

NARRATOR

Charlotte knows that Joan smokes. She pretends to have quit, but has smoked bi-annually ever since Charlotte can remember. But who is Charlotte to judge her mother's flaws?

Charlotte can count the amount of things she has done wrong in her life on one hand, and each time Joan had been there. Never telling Ray.

One being the time she took ecstasy, forgot how to speak English and watched the movie *Clueless* on repeat for six hours straight.

Two was the time she shoplifted a pair of socks when she was nine.

And three was when she gave her first blowjob and accidentally bit the young man's penis. Charlotte called her mother, who had to come tend to both of them.

This situation is different. Charlotte isn't in trouble. But she is in a crisis.

Joan knows something is going on with Charlotte but she doesn't know what. She thinks about this as she erases the traces of her cigarette.

There is a friendly banging on the door. JOAN *quickly stubs out her cigarette, rolls it up in some paper and pops it in a sandwich bag like a pro. She opens up a hollow book, pops in the bag and pulls out some perfume. She sprays it around. She then pulls out some breath spray, and sprays her mouth. Finally, she rubs some hand cream into her hands. She closes the hollow book and places it back.*

JOAN Francis! I think your parents are here!

JOAN *answers the door.* ROSE *runs in, throwing a huge hug around her mother.* SONNY *follows, lugging a huge amount of bags, but he's still chipper.*

ROSE Mum!

JOAN Rose! Sonny!

ROSE Mum! I missed you so much!

JOAN You're so brown!

ROSE Sonny took me on a surprise trip to Eden Roc at Cap Cana!

JOAN Where on earth is that?

SONNY *hugs* JOAN *and hands her a present.*

SONNY The Dominican Republic.

JOAN I've always wanted to go there!

SONNY If we had known, we would have taken you.

ROSE Oh, Mum, you would love it. LOVE. IT. Wouldn't she, Sonny?

SONNY Love it.

ROSE We had this villa right on the lagoon. And the water in there is so blue. Like no shade I've ever seen before. And every day we would just eat fruit and swim and drive our golf cart around the island. It was like that island in the Florida

Keys – remember? Except a resort. Just really private.

It was like being on a deserted island if that deserted island had staff and an infinity pool.

JOAN How delightful.

ROSE Mum, it was so good. I was just this sloth, eating tuna tartare, laying in the hammock and watching the sunset on Jaunillo Beach.

SONNY You should go.

JOAN Well, if your father ever takes me.

SONNY Forget Ray, come with us. I'd look great with two beautiful women by my side.

RAY *walks into the room with his virtual reality mask on, feeling his away around as if blind.*

ROSE Daddy! What on earth are you doing?!

RAY *takes off his mask.*

RAY If it isn't little Rosie-May and the big Blackfella!

SONNY Ray!

SONNY *and* RAY *hug.* RAY*'s demeanour to* SONNY *is the antithesis of his response to* FRANCIS

RAY How was LA?

ROSE Great. I'll have to be back again in January and then we'll open that store at the beginning of February. You'll have to come over. It's the most amazing space. It's, like, minimal, and the whole store is based around a pool.

JOAN Your store has a pool?

ROSE I call it a tranquil area for, like, thinking and reflecting.

JOAN You did always think big, my darling.

ROSE It's just this very minimal 70s holiday vibe. Lots of rock and green and neutrals and gray and glass.

RAY I have no idea what any of that means.

SONNY Neither do I. But take her word for it, it's great.

ROSE I mean, it's more of a space than a "store" anyway. Like, you can buy things, but it's more about the lifestyle choices you're making when you're in the space. I have pics on my phone. Here.

ROSE *pulls out her phone and hands it around.* CHARLOTTE *comes running in, with* FRANCIS *behind her.*

CHARLOTTE ROSIE-MAY!

ROSE CC! Why didn't you come visit us in Paris?

CHARLOTTE I couldn't, I was just / so busy

ROSE / Who's this?

CHARLOTTE This is Francis.

FRANCIS Hey, guys. I've heard so much about you. It's lovely to meet you.

ROSE This is Francis?

FRANCIS That's me!

ROSE Not quite what I expected.

CHARLOTTE What did you expect?

SONNY I expected somebody English.

"Like I'm from England, yeah. Chimney sweep, got a fiver." You know . . . because you met in London.

FRANCIS Ha, no, not English.

ROSE Well, you kind of are.

FRANCIS Pardon?

ROSE Well, where else are you from?

FRANCIS Australia.

ROSE But where are you from?

FRANCIS Uh, Sydney, specifically.

ROSE What's your background?

FRANCIS Australian?

ROSE But you're White.

FRANCIS That I am.

ROSE So where did your family come from?

CHARLOTTE Rose.

FRANCIS Yes, my family is traced back to the UK.

ROSE See, Sonny, you were right.

SONNY Don't worry, mate, my mum is White too.

CHARLOTTE Francis, this is my sister, Rose.

FRANCIS Lovely to meet you, Rose.

ROSE So this is the man who has stolen my sister away?

FRANCIS Just call me the Aborigines Protection Board.

Everyone is silent.

FRANCIS Like I stole . . . your sister . . . like the Stolen Generations . . .

CHARLOTTE Francis.

FRANCIS I'm sorry. It was a joke. Not the Stolen Generations, I'm sorry for that too.

ROSE Our grandmother was part of the stolen generations.

FRANCIS I'm so sorry.

ROSE Francis, is it? Francis, this is my husband, Sonny.

FRANCIS It is such a pleasure to meet you both. And, Sonny, my father is such a fan. As am I.

SONNY Mate, don't worry, that was years ago now.

FRANCIS Best player in the game.

SONNY Thank you. I replaced the footy boots with a suit a while ago now but it's always nice to know people still remember me.

RAY Remember you? You're a bloody legend.

Drinks?

ROSE Yes, please. Do we have any champagne?

CHARLOTTE Oh yes, bubbles!

JOAN There's a bottle of Bolly in the chiller.

RAY Sonny?

SONNY A beer would be great.

RAY Pilsner?

SONNY Perfect.

RAY Glass?

SONNY Thanks, Dad.

RAY No problemo.

JOAN Francis?

RAY I'm not the bloody waiter.

JOAN Yes, you are. Put yourself to good use. Think of it like virtual reality but in real life.

FRANCIS Beer, please.

ROSE *thrusts a box at* CHARLOTTE.

ROSE Here. I have a gift for you too, Char.

Open your gifts.

JOAN I'll save it for Christmas.

ROSE They aren't Christmas gifts, they're hello gifts. I haven't seen either of you for three and a half months. What kind of Blacks are we? Now, open your gifts.

JOAN *and* CHARLOTTE *open their gifts. In the boxes lay beautiful silver and turquoise Native American jewels.*

JOAN This is beautiful.

CHARLOTTE They remind me / of—

ROSE / Of New Mexico. After we got back from Palm Springs, Sonny and I decided to hire a car and take a road trip to Las Vegas instead of flying. We always fly.

SONNY I got a Ferrari. Vroom.

JOAN And how is your mum, Sonny?

SONNY She's getting there. The loss of Dad hit her pretty hard.

RAY *walks in balancing a tray of drinks, virtual reality mask sitting atop his head. Everybody takes a drink.*

RAY Your father was a good man, Sonny. Especially for a Jesus freak.

SONNY Speaking of Jesus / actually

ROSE / How good is it to be back here? And to see my family again. Do you have much family, Francis?

FRANCIS Not really, just my mum and dad.

ROSE Any siblings?

FRANCIS No, just me. That I know of.

ROSE You have siblings you don't know of?

FRANCIS I was just joking. Like, maybe my dad . . . cheated . . .

ROSE Your dad cheated?

FRANCIS I don't know.

SONNY Oh, yeah, get it! Like we could all have brothers and sisters that we don't know of.

I wonder if the show will find any siblings I never knew I had.

RAY Ah, yes! The show! How did filming go, Sonny? You know, if you weren't married to Rose I'd be pretty happy if you found out you were related to me!

SONNY Thankfully I'm pretty sure I'm not.

RAY You never know!

FRANCIS You know, you do look alike.

ROSE Yep, all us Blackfellas look the same.

RAY Could you imagine, me and the big fella, the political leader and the footy player?

Now that would make a great show.

JOAN Raymond, please, you're giving your ego a boner.

RAY I am not! I am just proud of our family.

Let's have a toast. To the five of us!

JOAN Six of us, Raymond. Six.

RAY To our family coming back together for our first Christmas in two years. To hope and to faith. As Martin Luther King said: "Faith is taking the first step even when you don't see the whole staircase." Go the mob!

EVERYONE Go the mob!

RAY leads SONNY and FRANCIS out for their initiation into the family. JOAN, CHARLOTTE and ROSE start to put together the Christmas tree and decorate it.

NARRATOR

Sonny is a wealthy banker, but most importantly, Sonny is a retired football star. One of the best players of all time and, many say, the most famous Aboriginal football player to date.

Sonny didn't grow up wealthy like Rose. He was raised in the Western Suburbs of Sydney by a school teacher and a preacher. He got an Aboriginal rugby union scholarship to a private all-boys school. He met Rose at the school dance between St Jude's and the Lady of the Christ at Lavender Bay.

They consummated their relationship straight away, at age 16, in the school toilets. The one with the faulty lock and the graffiti that said "Lucy Albatross is a Fat Slut".

They've been in love ever since.

It was when Sonny's dad died that he first heard the voice of the Lord.

Sonny realised that no matter what happened here on earth, the true father, the one father, was the father who had sent his son, Jesus Christ, to die for us on earth. And that the Son of the Lord is always there for you. No matter what.

Sonny has also been filming for *Celebrity: Where Do You Come From?*, which has been tracing back his family history.

He doesn't know it yet, but soon he will get a call from the show that will change his and Rose's lives forever.

SCENE 4

ROSE *and* CHARLOTTE *play Mariah Carey's Christmas album and decorate the Christmas tree.* ROSE *pulls a joint out of her purse and lights it. She takes a big inhale.*

ROSE To Christmas traditions!

CHARLOTTE What about your newfound born-again beliefs?

ROSE *passes the joint to* CHARLOTTE, *who takes a smoke. They pass the joint back and forth.*

ROSE It's helping Sonny deal with the death of his father, so if I have to "praise be the lord" a few times to make sure he's okay, so be it.

CHARLOTTE Are you saying it's all a show?

ROSE It's not a show. I do believe in God. I'm just an antagonist.

CHARLOTTE Antagonist?

ROSE Yeah, like, I believe in *a* god, I just don't know who. Or what. Or where. I do think whatever God is, it's definitely a woman.

CHARLOTTE You mean agnostic.

ROSE What?

CHARLOTTE Antagonist is a bad guy.

ROSE Oh, okay. I'm sorry. Sorry I'm the dumb daughter.

CHARLOTTE Don't do that.

ROSE I'm just some silly little fashion designer and you're the world-class lawyer and social commentator.

CHARLOTTE You're smart enough to charge $580 for a t-shirt.

ROSE Or some people are just stupid enough to buy a $580 t-shirt.

Charlotte, you like Francis a lot?

CHARLOTTE I love him.

ROSE For how long?

CHARLOTTE What do you mean?

ROSE You can do the holier than thou thing for Mum and Dad, Char, but I see you. I SEE YOU, you big ol' slut. How serious are you?

CHARLOTTE Oh, come on.

ROSE You're serious enough to bring him here for Christmas, so that's pretty serious.

CHARLOTTE There's something I should tell you.

ROSE You're pregnant?!

CHARLOTTE No!

ROSE Thank God.

CHARLOTTE What do you mean, "Thank God?"

ROSE It's probably good you're not. I mean, how long how you known Francis? Three months?

CHARLOTTE I resent that.

ROSE How long then?

CHARLOTTE . . .

ROSE How long?

CHARLOTTE . . . Three months and two weeks and four days. Do you not like Francis?

ROSE No, of course I do. He's great.

I just . . . I just . . . look, no, he's great.

CHARLOTTE Look what? What's wrong?

ROSE If you google Australian Aboriginal mixed race, do you know the first thing that comes up?

CHARLOTTE What?

ROSE The Stolen Generations.

CHARLOTTE Oh, come on.

ROSE It's true. Google the Stolen Generations. Think about that.

CHARLOTTE Is this about his Stolen Generations joke? Because he didn't mean that. He's just bad at making jokes.

ROSE Have you ever even dated a Black man, Charlotte?

CHARLOTTE I dated Tyson. You know Tyson?

ROSE Ted Turner's son? The doctor?

CHARLOTTE Yeah.

ROSE Isn't he our cousin?!

CHARLOTTE I didn't know that at the time!

I mean, I purposely didn't ask.

But then one night in bed, after, you know, he asked if I was a Gibson Gibson from out this way. We did the math, we were cousins.

ROSE Gross.

CHARLOTTE Can't get pregnant up the bum.

ROSE Charlotte! Too much!

CHARLOTTE Wait. What if I am so stoned I think I'm talking to Rose and I'm actually talking to Dad? And I just told Dad I had bum sex.

ROSE I'm Rose.

Wait.

No, I'm Rose.

What did Daddy say about Francis?

CHARLOTTE It's less about Francis and more about him wanting me to take this TV gig.

To further my career. Or his career.

ROSE Or both?

CHARLOTTE Who cares?

ROSE He does, obviously.

CHARLOTTE He is so intense about this idea of a legacy he has for this family as, like, Aboriginal leaders.

ROSE I wish Daddy showed the same level of enthusiasm for my career.

CHARLOTTE That last case I did has really . . .

Don't you ever feel guilty about the fact we have so much?

ROSE No.

CHARLOTTE Come on. You don't feel uncomfortable about being a well-known Aboriginal person and yet we, you and I, have never struggled?

ROSE Struggle isn't Aboriginality. That's poverty porn.

CHARLOTTE I'm just saying maybe our experience may not be indicative of a broader community.

ROSE What: we can't have different kinds of Black people?

CHARLOTTE No, that's not my point. If our Blackness is a lived experience, and the majority of Black people aren't privy to the privileges we have, then can we really call ourselves Black?

ROSE Look, no matter if Sonny or I make six or seven figures a year—

CHARLOTTE Both of those sums are above the average wage.

ROSE The point is, no matter how much money Sonny or I make, we are still Black. Class and race are not the same thing, Char. Don't get it twisted.

CHARLOTTE I'm not saying we're not Black. If race is constructed and culture is lived, then if we're rich, then maybe our culture is changing?

ROSE So you're saying we're coconuts?

CHARLOTTE That's not what I'm saying. I'm talking about the arbitration of racial identity and socio-economic class.

ROSE Do you always have to say what I say but smarter?

CHARLOTTE It's not what you said.

ROSE How much does Francis make a year?

CHARLOTTE Rose, that's inappropriate.

ROSE Oh my God, who's acting White now? Char, how much does he make? Thirty grand a year tops?

CHARLOTTE His money doesn't matter to me.

ROSE Because you have it!

My point is, you can't judge my race because of my money or class. Because if you can, then Francis is Blacker than all of us.

CHARLOTTE Rose, I read one of Dad's early speeches this year. Like, one of his first ones ever.

About the construction of race and cultural genocide. He defined Whiteness as a value system, one that is also radicalised by class. Essentially, the more you attain those values, the closer to White you are. That's cultural genocide.

He said that. Our father.

ROSE So anyone rich and ethnic are the new White? What are poor Whites then: the new Blacks?

CHARLOTTE That's not what I'm saying.

ROSE Your argument makes no sense, Char.

CHARLOTTE As long as you're Black, you're Black?

ROSE Yep.

CHARLOTTE And those who look less Black?

ROSE Look less Black, but are still Black.

It's about community recognition and being part of your people.

Sonny and I are going to have big Black babies. This I know. And they're going to be beautiful and Black and proud. And they'll probably wear Burberry.

CHARLOTTE You sound like a Kardashian.

ROSE You know, that doesn't offend me at all. It's a compliment.

Char, let me be clear.

What I'm saying is, think about the consequences if you were to have a future with Francis. What that would look like . . . fully.

Shit, Mum's coming!

NARRATOR

Rose knows that her mother knows she smokes pot, but to humour Charlotte she pretends that their mother has no idea. She enjoys knowing things that Charlotte doesn't.

For some reason she could never quite understand, Rose was always considered the more "artistic" child. Which we all know means the less intelligent one.

ROSE Hey!

CHARLOTTE I didn't say anything.

NARRATOR

Which isn't true at all, because Rose spends a lot of time doing online IQ tests and she always scores well above average.

Rose dropped out of two university courses before entering the fashion business, in which she has been very successful. She attributes her success in business to a fearlessness that is typical in Scorpios.

Although she is fearless, Rose does have bad dreams. When she was a little girl, her grandmother told her about how they would hide from the Aborigines Protection Board.

Ever since then she has had the same dream: that she is in her childhood bedroom, looking outside a window and watching her family being driven away. She screams for the car to stop, but it doesn't. She keeps screaming, louder and louder, as she watches her family being stolen. Very often Rose wakes up crying, missing her family as if they were already gone.

Rose tells everybody she wants nothing more than a big Black family. Her and Sonny have been trying for many months now. At least Sonny thinks so. But Rose is secretly still taking the pill. She doesn't know why.

Right now Rose is wondering how much longer she can keep hiding it from Sonny.

And as she thinks about this, she can't help thinking about that dream.

CHARLOTTE *and* ROSE *repeat the same process* JOAN *did earlier.* JOAN *walks in carrying a box with more decorations.*

JOAN The tree looks beautiful. I haven't had my girls decorate the Christmas tree for me in years.

ROSE It was two Christmases ago, Mum.

JOAN In Aboriginal years, with our life expectancy, two years is like 6.4 non-Aboriginal years.

ROSE *gives her mum a hug.*

ROSE I missed you.

JOAN Both of you, come here. I bet you missed your mama.

JOAN *starts pulling things out of the box.*

JOAN Here are your stockings that you've had since you were little girls.

CHARLOTTE I love how you tell us this as if we haven't heard it before.

ROSE Or if it wasn't, like, you know, our lives.

JOAN I don't have grandchildren, so until I get them, my babies will be my babies forever.

ROSE I have a feeling that won't change even if you get grandchildren.

JOAN Probably not.

So who's going to turn on the lights?

CHARLOTTE Rose can.

ROSE *turns on the Christmas tree lights.* JOAN *pulls both her daughters in tight. They are together and in awe.*

JOAN I love you both. Very much.

Also, just so you girls know, marijuana has been shown to lower fertility in females.

JOAN *leaves.*

CHARLOTTE Think she knows?

ROSE Think she knows what?

CHARLOTTE That we're high?

ROSE Stop being paranoid.

SCENE 5

RAY, JOAN, CHARLOTTE, FRANCIS, ROSE *and* SONNY *sit around the Christmas tree, eating from charcuterie boards.*

RAY I'm gonna bloody well fall asleep if these fellas don't get here soon.

JOAN Well, Ray, just go to sleep, then.

RAY I'm articulating a point.

FRANCIS I'm really very sorry. Maybe we should just start without them?

CHARLOTTE Of course not. We can't start Kris Kringle without your parents.

ROSE They also have two of the presents, so do the math.

JOAN It's fine, really, Francis. Ray is just being dramatic.

RAY It'll be Christmas before they get here.

JOAN When were they meant to arrive again, Francis?

FRANCIS Uh, this morning . . .

JOAN This morning?! Are they okay?

RAY You know who's not okay? Me.

JOAN You are definitely not okay.

SONNY How about I prepare some drinks. Any requests from the cellar?

ROSE Oh – that wine Daddy gets from Argentina.

RAY The Malbec.

SONNY So, bottle of the Malbec?

JOAN Make it two . . . three.

SONNY Okey dokey.

SONNY *leaves.* CHARLOTTE *pulls* FRANCIS *aside.*

CHARLOTTE Your parents are coming, aren't they, Franny?

FRANCIS Of course.

CHARLOTTE And you did tell them where to come, right?

FRANCIS Oh, yeah, I totally told them where to go.

CHARLOTTE With clear instructions?

FRANCIS Really clear.

CHARLOTTE And how did you tell them?

FRANCIS Phone.

CHARLOTTE Just phone?

FRANCIS And text.

CHARLOTTE Show me.

FRANCIS What?

CHARLOTTE Show me your phone. I want to see the texts.

FRANCIS You don't trust me.

CHARLOTTE Darling, of course I do . . .

CHARLOTTE *quickly reaches into* FRANCIS's *back pocket and takes the phone. She starts scrolling through it.*

CHARLOTTE Francis! Twelve missed calls!

FRANCIS I must have had my phone . . . on . . . quiet.

CHARLOTTE More like you must have had your phone on avoid.

FRANCIS Okay, yes. I had my phone on avoid.

Charlotte, this is a terrible idea.

CHARLOTTE You gave them the wrong address! In the wrong town!

FRANCIS I was desperate.

CHARLOTTE Francis, they have to meet at some point.

FRANCIS But why now? Your father can barely stand me; the spawn of his nemesis /

CHARLOTTE / My father can barely stand anyone. They're going to have to meet. Remember? It's like a bandaid. Just pull / it off quick.

FRANCIS / Pull it off quick.

CHARLOTE Yes. What happened to the bandaid, Francis?

FRANCIS I don't think the scab is ready yet.

CHARLOTTE The scab meaning you.

FRANCIS The scab meaning me.

CHARLOTTE It has to come off. Every wound needs air . . . Okay, enough with the metaphor.

Francis, they need to meet at some point. Do you want them to meet at the wedding?

FRANCIS But why at Christmas?

CHARLOTTE Because no one can be mad at Christmas. We talked about this.

FRANCIS I don't know how it is for your people, but for us Whites, historically Christmas is a time where everyone gets mad at each other. In fact, that's what Christmas is known for: coming together with people who piss you off to whom you just happen to have a genetic connection.

CHARLOTTE *scrolls through the phone.*

CHARLOTTE Yeah, look, that's pretty similar for Black people too.

JOAN *and* ROSE *call from across the room.*

JOAN Charlotte! Francis! Come over and taste this cheese! It's divine.

ROSE It has truffles.

CHARLOTTE *shoves the phone into* FRANCIS's *hand.*

CHARLOTTE Call your parents now.

CHARLOTTE *walks over to her family.* FRANCIS *slowly dials his parents and holds the phone to his ear. It rings. And rings. It goes to voicemail.*

RAY That bloody Dennison just tweeted the stupidest thing. Again. He said that / salad

JOAN / Ray!

FRANCIS I tried calling them but it rang out. Maybe we should just start without them?

RAY Yes. Yes, let's start right away.

JOAN Ray!

CHARLOTTE Francis, what's going / on

FRANCIS / Great, let's start. Here, let me get the gifts—

There is a knock at the door.

JOAN Maybe that's your parents, Francis?

RAY About time.

JOAN *walks towards the door.*

FRANCIS No, let me get that /

JOAN / Don't be silly, it's fine.

JOAN *opens the door with flourish and stops suddenly. In the doorway stand* DENNISON *and* MARIE. MARIE *is holding beautifully wrapped gifts.*

DENNISON For Chrissakes, Marie, we're probably at the wrong bloody place again! *(looks at his phone)* That dickhead tweeted me!

MARIE Dennison—

DENNISON Is that boy answering his phone – I barely even get reception out here in the bloody / bush.

MARIE / Dennison!

FRANCIS Mum. Dad. Merry Christmas.

MARIE My little boy, I haven't seen you since London.

FRANCIS Uh . . . these are my parents.

Mum, Dad, meet Raymond and / Joan.

DENNISON / we know who they are.

RAY You! What are you doing here?!

DENNISON What are you doing here?

RAY What am I doing here? What are you doing here!?

DENNISON More like what are you doing here?

RAY I said, what are you doing here!?

DENNISON That's what I asked you!

RAY I asked you first!

DENNISON Well, then, what are you doing here?!

RAY I asked you second! What are you . . . Goddammit! This is my house! That's what I'm doing here! Now get out, you White, foul-smelling / bigot!

JOAN / Raymond! Stop!

DENNISON That's it, I'm leaving.

MARIE Dennison, don't you dare.

RAY Good riddance!

DENNISON I'm not being disrespected like this.

RAY Ha! You're not being respected at all to even be disrespected like this!

DENNISON That doesn't make any sense!

RAY Just like your career!

JOAN Raymond!

RAY Charlotte, is this a joke? The son of Dennison Smith?

CHARLOTTE It's not a joke, Dad.

RAY Dennison Smith. Dennison Bloody Smith.

DENNISON Yes, Dennison Smith, that's my name.

RAY I'm not talking to you!

Dennison Smith the right-wing Liberal racist bigot who tried to ruin my career.

You're seriously bringing him and his spawn into my house?

CHARLOTTE Yes.

FRANCIS Look, I'm as pleased as anyone that I'm his spawn.

DENNISON *points to* RAY

DENNISON What about him?!

RAY What about me?

DENNISON It's so rich! You calling me the right-wing racist bigot who ruins careers. You, who pointed out my race and called me White as soon as I stepped foot in this house! Maybe I wouldn't have been a bigot if you didn't constantly throw the race card at me!

RAY The race card? You even dare to say that! Here?! Under a Black man's roof!

DENNISON There we go! The race card again! Putting words into my mouth! Why can't you just call it a roof!

RAY Get out!

CHARLOTTE Dad!

DENNISON With pleasure.

DENNISON *walks towards the door.* MARIE *stands in front of it.*

MARIE You are not going anywhere.

JOAN Raymond. Stop it. Stop it now.

CHARLOTTE Maybe we should try this again?

MARIE Good idea.

CHARLOTTE It's so lovely to finally meet you, Marie. Is it Ma*rie* or *Ma*rie?

MARIE Ma*rie*. Thank you for asking, darling.

CHARLOTTE I've heard so many good things about you.

Lovely to meet you properly, Dennison.

JOAN And lovely to see you again after all these years, Marie. And you, Dennison.

JOAN *gives* MARIE *and* DENNISON *a cordial hug. She silently motions to* RAY. RAY *ignores her.*

JOAN Ray, shake his hand.

RAY No.

JOAN Raymond . . .

RAY No.

JOAN Shake his bloody hand.

They shake hands.

RAY Dennison.

DENNISON Raymond.

JOAN Please, make yourself at home.

MARIE You have a beautiful house.

JOAN Thank you.

RAY This land is our ancestral land.

MARIE Who are your people?

RAY The Gomeroi People.

DENNISON *scoffs.*

RAY Oi! You! Come over here and say that!

DENNISON I didn't say anything!

RAY Yes, you did!

DENNISON Oh, yeah! Prove it!

RAY You prove it!

DENNISON No, you prove it!

RAY I don't have to prove anything! This is my land!

SONNY *walks up the stairs whistling a tune, completely oblivious to what has gone on. He walks right into the tension.*

SONNY So there were a ton of Malbecs and I couldn't really tell the difference, so I just grabbed whatever. I mean, the more the merrier, right? . . . Oh. Hello! I'm Sonny. Merry Christmas!

SONNY *puts out his hand. No one takes it.*

SONNY Malbec Merlot anyone? It's from Argentina.

SCENE 6

NARRATOR

The antagonism between Ray Gibson and Dennison Smith was never perceived by others as the great rivalry it was in their own minds.

They were political opponents during the naughty nineties when Australian politics was on the brink of great social change and the landscape was dotted with ideological egos.

Ray Gibson was the handsome, charismatic Aboriginal politician with a great head of hair, who was at one point being touted as the future leader of the Labor Party. Dennison Smith was the dour, conservative social services minister for the Liberal Party who wore very expensive suits and had ambitions for the prime ministership that were supported by no one.

Neither can quite remember the exact moment when they became enemies, but their rivalry peaked when Ray threw his shoe across the floor at Dennison. Dennison tried to have Ray thrown out of parliament but no one cared.

Throughout their husbands' tumultuous years as political rivals, Marie and Joan managed to maintain a civil acquaintance mainly thanks to the enthusiasm of Marie, who was always very, very, very fond of Joan.

Marie Smith has recently come to a very big revelation about herself that she is yet to reveal to anyone. Especially Dennison. She plans to tell him on New Year's Eve. After this Christmas. The first they have spent with their son, Francis, in six years . . . That's 19.2 Aboriginal years.

MARIE Do you mind if I get the Wi-Fi password?

JOAN It's koori123.

CHARLOTTE You should really change that password.

DENNISON What do you need that for, Marie?

ROSE If anyone wants a tipple, there's eggnog that can come with a slosh of brandy.

Or sloshes, plural, if so desired.

DENNISON So, Sonny, what do your parents do?

SONNY My mother was a teacher. My father is a preacher. Used to be, he's passed now.

MARIE Oh, I'm sorry.

DENNISON I am very sorry to hear that.

JOAN It was very sudden.

RAY Sonny is doing the right thing, though, and tracing back his family roots.

MARIE How are you doing that?

ROSE You know that show where they trace back a celebrity's past and where they're from? Sonny's doing that.

SONNY My dad was Aboriginal but my mum is White. I really wanted to find out more about my mum's White side.

ROSE No idea why.

DENNISON White people's history and culture is just as important as anyone else's.

ROSE Yeah, we know. We live in it.

DENNISON Aside from the antsy pantsy TV stuff, back in the real world, how are you finding JP Morgan Chase, Sonny?

SONNY Oh, you know how it is. Work's work but the opportunities I've been afforded have been great.

DENNISON Do you know Stan Ferguson?

SONNY In legal?

DENNISON Head of.

SONNY I do! Great man.

ROSE How could you not tell me that Dennison Smith was Francis's father?

CHARLOTTE Because you have a big mouth.

ROSE Are you crazy bringing them here? They will kill each other in the night. And Dennison's an old racist.

CHARLOTTE You're exaggerating.

FRANCIS No, I don't think she is. She's right. He is old. And a racist.

ROSE It's your fault, too. They're going to kill each other.

FRANCIS We'll be lucky if they even wait till night. I'm surprised one hasn't glassed the other yet.

CHARLOTTE Look at Dad's eyes, he's totally thinking about it.

FRANCIS Sonny likes him.

ROSE So what? Sonny's a soft touch. He once cried during a dog food commercial.

DENNISON Ferguson has been a friend of the family since we were Rhodes scholars together.

We were there with Tony.

FRANCIS Christ, here we go.

DENNISON Very, very, very good friend of the family. Isn't that right, Marie?

MARIE Oh, yeah. Sure.

Joan, the eggnog is delicious. Did you make it?

JOAN I did.

MARIE Amazing!

JOAN I can give you the recipe.

MARIE Oh, no, don't waste your time. I'm a terrible cook. Even when it comes to liquids.

I'm only good at drinking them.

JOAN I'm sure that isn't true.

MARIE Oh, I'm not exaggerating. I really just cannot cook.

But maybe you can show me while we are here?

MARIE *grazes her hand across* JOAN's

JOAN Uh, sure. Maybe we could start with something small?

MARIE Do you know this is our first Christmas with Francis in years? Thank you so much, Charlotte, for getting him to stop avoiding me.

You must be a brilliant lawyer to have won that fight.

RAY She is. She is a brilliant lawyer. Francis is a very fortunate man.

FRANCIS I am indeed.

RAY One could even say he is punching above his weight.

FRANCIS I think any man would be punching out of their league when it came to Char.

DENNISON Well, Ray certainly punched above his weight with Joan. This eggnog is delicious.

Maybe now that Francis is getting serious about Charlotte, he may consider getting serious about the other things in his life.

MARIE Dennison, please.

DENNISON You know, Christmas isn't the only time of "giving" for Francis, unfortunately.

MARIE But this Christmas is the first in a long time that we have gotten Francis. And that gift is invaluable.

FRANCIS Thank you, / Mother.

DENNISON / Well, actually, I wouldn't say it was "invaluable" because we have paid a price. You see, there is always a price to be paid when it comes to Francis. You never leave with a full wallet.

FRANCIS You know, I really thought you would at least wait until Christmas Day when you were pissed and incompetent to start on / this.

CHARLOTTE / Do you know when Francis and I first met he serenaded me in the street?

MARIE What? My little Francis?

CHARLOTTE Yes. It had been a terrible date. Terrible, just really terrible. Like words can't even describe how terrible this date was.

RAY Ever heard the saying first impressions are usually the right / ones?

CHARLOTTE / We had been talking on Tinder for months / and—

ROSE / Oh, my God! You met on Tinder?! You never told me that. Shame!

MARIE Oh, that's not shameful! Lots of people are doing it these days. My podiatrist met his partner on Grindr.

CHARLOTTE See! So we're on this date and Francis has no money and he smells slightly strange.

Like vinegar.

FRANCIS I really have no idea what that was about.

CHARLOTTE And the conversation is just terrible. I thought, I can put up with no money. I can even put up with a strange smell. But terrible conversation? No. Just nope.

FRANCIS The thing was, I was just so intimidated by her. She was so smart and competent.

And she smelt good. And, look, to be fair, I was very aware of my vinegar smell.

SONNY Why did you smell like vinegar?

FRANCIS Oh, well . . . uh . . .

DENNISON Yes, Francis. Why?

CHARLOTTE Oh, look, he really didn't smell that badly of vinegar. I was exaggerating the story.

FRANCIS You know what they say, when the fact becomes legend, print the legend.

ROSE Someone printed that you smelt like vinegar?

FRANCIS Uh, no, it's just a saying.

DENNISON No, when I saw you in London, I do remember the distinct smell of vinegar.

FRANCIS Alright, to be completely honest, I had an infection in my sweat glands. And I distinctly remember you didn't smell too good yourself.

DENNISON Francis, really.

FRANCIS It's called propionibacterium and it's nothing to be ashamed of. It breaks down the amino acids in your sweat glands into propionic acid, which causes the vinegar smell. It's a perfectly natural medical illness.

CHARLOTTE You never told me that.

FRANCIS I saw a doctor one day when you were working.

JOAN Well, you know what they say: true love is blind. That must, uh, extend to smell.

CHARLOTTE Anyways, back to the story, I walked out onto the street, completely devastated about this terrible date and then all of a sudden, Francis comes running out with his huge cello. He sets it up and he starts playing— /

FRANCIS / "Mysterious Girl", Peter Andre. She had said it was her favourite secret song.

CHARLOTTE I knew I was in love.

FRANCIS I knew I loved her from the moment I saw her.

SONNY *wipes tears away.*

SONNY That's beautiful. Just really, really beautiful.

ROSE That's cute.

And lame. Really lame.

JOAN Sounds like our Charlotte might be the lucky one here.

MARIE Francis has always been such a sweet boy. Very sensitive and sweet. One time he got so scared watching the film *Jaws* he wet himself.

FRANCIS Mother, really.

DENNISON You really do have a beautiful property out here.

RAY Thank you. It's our ancestral land.

DENNISON *snorts.*

DENNISON And did your ancestral land come with the mansion or not?

RAY Excuse me?

DENNISON Just saying it's a very flash humpee you have here.

RAY Here, you better look out! I let you into this flash humpee and I can kick you out of it.

DENNISON What? Gonna spear me too?

RAY Yeah, and I know exactly where I would, you racist.

DENNISON Settle down, settle down, Gibbo. Just having a joke with you.

MARIE So, Charlotte, I'm sure your parents' work has played a role in your career today?

CHARLOTTE Oh, I'm constantly getting introduced as Ray Gibson's daughter. The shadow I can't escape.

JOAN I'm sorry, darling, that's terrible.

RAY Uh . . . why is that terrible? Why is being introduced as Ray Gibson's daughter terrible?

CHARLOTTE It's not being introduced as your daughter, Dad. It's being reduced to being your daughter. All the time.

FRANCIS You should try being reduced to Ray Gibson's daughter's boyfriend!

RAY What?

FRANCIS Look, it's not . . . a bad thing . . . at all . . . I'm really happy to be joining this family. This beautiful . . . multicultural family. It's an honour. You know . . . like that song . . . "Ebony and Ivory" . . . you know, that song—

FRANCIS *starts singing lyrics to the Paul McCartney classic "Ebony and Ivory".*

FRANCIS "Ebony and ivory, live together in perfect harmony . . . ooh."

CHARLOTTE Oh, god.

MARIE Isn't Francis so gifted?

FRANCIS Mother, please. I was just joking. You know . . . being self-deprecating.

Like I'm a great white hand bag.

DENNISON A hand bag? Francis, if you could just hear the way you're talking about yourself.

Have some pride.

ROSE White pride? That always ends well.

RAY What's wrong with being a woman's hand bag? Are you not a feminist? Sometimes being a hand bag is what's needed to truly support a woman. /

DENNISON / Equality is not about reducing people to hand bags. That was always your problem, Gibson, you were never consistent /

RAY Never consistent!

SONNY Rose makes brilliant hand bags. I always joke about how great it would be if men could carry hand bags. That's like the last obstacle of sexism, isn't it? For men to do femme things without being mocked?

FRANCIS *starts singing again.*

FRANCIS "Ebony and ivory, live together in perfect / harmony . . ."

SONNY Please, Francis, I'm rooting for you. Stop singing.

FRANCIS Oh, God, I'm making it worse.

Look, I love being a Black woman's white hand bag. Love it.

RAY What? Black woman?

FRANCIS I mean, love that I'm going to be your future son-in-law.

JOAN Son-in-law?

CHARLOTTE Francis!

RAY My son-in-law?

FRANCIS What I mean is, that you're Black and I'm White and that's great . . . Look, what I'm saying is that most of all I love that I'm going to be Charlotte's husband.

JOAN You're engaged?!

MARIE Congratulations!

CHARLOTTE Francis wasn't meant to tell you. We were waiting to see how this went.

MARIE Congratulations!

JOAN Yes, congratulations! Welcome to the family, Francis.

DENNISON Are you sure?

CHARLOTTE Excuse me?

FRANCIS What do you mean, are we sure?

DENNISON Are either of you sure about this?

CHARLOTTE Uh – we are very sure / about

FRANCIS Dad, do not. Please.

RAY What are you talking about? Because Charlotte's Black?

JOAN Raymond!

DENNISON Francis, you can barely support yourself, let alone someone else.

MARIE Dennison, stop it!

CHARLOTTE He does not need to support me, and if needed I can support him.

RAY I didn't raise you to support a White boy!

FRANCIS Okay, this is humiliating.

CHARLOTTE My fiancé!

ROSE Char . . . Really? It's only been three months.

CHARLOTTE This is what I tried to tell you earlier. In private.

ROSE Have you really thought about this?

FRANCIS Of course we have thought about it.

ROSE But / really—

JOAN / You're engaged!

SONNY Cheers to the happy couple!

They cheer.

MARIE / Joan, do mothers-in-law become sisters? Maybe some kind of Aboriginal way?

JOAN Well, actually, in my people's culture the kinship / system—

RAY / Anyone want to watch my speech?

ROSE Dad, we've already watched it. On TV. On YouTube. On my phone on YouTube. On the podcast. On the app.

SONNY It was really inspiring.

RAY Over a million views on YouTube.

JOAN They were mostly your father.

DENNISON You know, you can pay Indians $5 to give you a million likes on anything this day and age. Tony did it. Backfired, though.

RAY You know what they're calling me?

JOAN Not this again, Ray. Celebratory drinks, anyone?

JOAN *pours herself a drink.*

RAY Martin Luther King.

That is what they're calling me.

DENNISON For God's sake.

RAY What?

DENNISON You're really comparing yourself to Doctor King?

MARIE I might refresh my . . . refreshment.

RAY I'm not calling myself that, the people are.

DENNISON You just believe whatever people tell you?

RAY If enough people agree. That's democracy.

DENNISON No, that's just the internet.

RAY Not just the internet when you're getting torn to shreds about lettuce.

Shit, I should have tweeted that instead.

DENNISON You had people calling me Hitler.

RAY Your comments about rocket being better than iceberg were fascist and racist.

DENNISON A Nazi!

RAY If the shoe fits.

DENNISON You have got to be kidding me.

RAY Here we go again. Australia's least formidable political opponent. Is there ever a time in your life where you haven't compensated for doing nothing by attacking someone?

DENNISON You gave a speech.

RAY It was a commentary!

DENNISON Dr Martin Luther King got shot.

RAY Yeah, and?

DENNISON Well, maybe if you keep making the comparison . . .

RAY Excuse me?

DENNISON You might actually have to commit to your values wholeheartedly for once in your life.

SONNY Music! Music. Let's put on some music.

FRANCIS I have a new composition I can play.

CHARLOTTE Yes, it's brilliant! Francis, get your cello. He is so good!

RAY I'm going to do what I should have done all those years in parliament and those White bastards stopped me. I'm gonna punch— /

DENNISON / Oh, yeah, Ray. Those White bastards really did you in. You haven't benefited at all.

RAY At least I've worked for what I've got.

DENNISON Debatable.

SONNY How about dancing?

CHARLOTTE Yes! Dancing!

SONNY *puts on a 70s disco tune, like "He's the Greatest Dancer", "It's Raining Men", "Kung Fu Fighting" or "Disco Inferno". Everyone starts dancing, trying to distract* RAY *and* DENNISON *from each other. The men continue to fight as they get pulled into dancing.*

DENNISON You were only successful because of two things: you were Black and you had hair!

RAY What did my hair have to do with anything?!

DENNISON It has everything to do with it! Ray, the Aboriginal man with the good hair couldn't take a step wrong. Never mind you were fiscally irresponsible and relied on buzzwords!

RAY You had no buzzwords! I was the Aboriginal leader this country needed.

DENNISON You were token!

RAY Ha! That's what you Libs love to say.

DENNISON It was all hair and buzzwords! The entire 90s!

RAY You crazy old kook.

DENNISON Calling me an old kook? I'm not the old man on Twitter trying to be relevant again.

RAY You're on Twitter, too!

DENNISON I'm not the one thinking they're the second coming of the civil rights movement!

RAY Because no one gives a shit what you say!

DENNISON Yes, they do!

RAY Why would anyone, in 2018, care about what an old racist has to say? You are IRRELEVANT.

DENNISON Me?! NO! YOU ARE IRRELEVANT!

RAY / Good luck! Look at you. Pathetic. You can't even dance.

DENNISON What's . . . what's this, then?

DENNISON *does some outdated dance move.*

RAY Pathetic!

RAY *does a dance move.* RAY *and* DENNISON *start a dance-off. Each one is more outdated and preposterous than the other. They both start to sweat and turn red.*

NARRATOR

As Charlotte watched her father dance, she wondered if this is where he thought he would end up when he first read the words of Martin Luther King.

Blackout.

SCENE 7

CHRISTMAS DAY

The sun comes up through the room. FRANCIS *plays his cello.* CHARLOTTE *comes out with a cup of coffee and watches him. The sun comes up, and as it does everyone sets up the Christmas lunch setting. It's beautiful. Dishes of food lay spread, the food smells delicious and bottles of champagne are scattered about within easy reach of everyone. Everyone sits around the table. They are pulling on Christmas crackers. Some have already been opened, and some of them are wearing paper Christmas crowns.* RAY *and* DENNISON *are sulking. Everyone ignores them.*

ROSE Mum, where did you get these? It's like trying to tear rubber.

JOAN David Joneses.

ROSE David Jones.

JOAN David Joneses.

CHARLOTTE David Jones.

JOAN David Joneses.

ROSE Mum, I can't believe after all these years you still can't say David Jones right.

JOAN Well, you know what they say: you can take the girl out of the country but you can't take the country out of the girl.

ROSE You're wearing Prada.

JOAN Prada's actually Aboriginal. It's pronounced, "Praadaa".

MARIE Really? I thought it was Italian.

JOAN Oh, no, it's Italian.

MARIE So Prada isn't Aboriginal?

CHARLOTTE It's a joke we have.

MARIE And the crackers, they're not Prada?

JOAN No, they're from / David Joneses.

ROSE/CHARLOTTE David Joneses.

ROSE/CHARLOTTE Jinx!

MARIE Oh! It's actually pronounced David Jones. *(pulling cracker)*

And wherever these are from, they are very good quality!

MARIE'S *arm flies back, nearly knocking whoever she's sitting next to in the head.*

MARIE They are tough. Here, Dennison. You can wear the hat.

MARIE *tosses* DENNISON *the hat.*

ROSE What does the joke say?

MARIE Why did the policeman smell bad?

ROSE Why?

MARIE He was on duty.

ROSE I don't get it. On duty? Duty . . . duty . . . duty?
What kind of jokes are these?
Charlotte?

CHARLOTTE What's Beethoven's favourite fruit?

ROSE What?

CHARLOTTE Ba. Na-na-naaa. Ba-na. Na. Naa.

ROSE What is that?

CHARLOTTE Ba-na-na. Naa. I don't / get

ROSE / What are you even saying?

CHARLOTTE I don't get it. Francis?

FRANCIS Oh, I got it. Ba-na-na-naaaaaa. As in, you know, "Ba-na-na-na. Ba-na-na-na. Ba-nana-na. Ba-na-na-na. Ba-na-na-na. Ba-na-na-na. Ba-na-na-na."

SONNY *joins in.*

FRANCIS/
SONNY Ba-na-na-naaaaaa! Ba-na-na-naaaaaa! Ba-na-na-na! Na! Naaaaaa!

SONNY *and* FRANCIS *high five.*

JOAN That's the worse joke I've ever heard and I'm married to Ray.

ROSE Yes, these jokes are terrible.

MARIE I do have to say, this looks amazing. A feast, if you will. Wouldn't you agree,

Dennison?

DENNISON Hmph.

MARIE You are the full package, Joan. Smart, beautiful, caring, intelligent, a great chef, in great shape, funny, beautiful. Stunningly beautiful, really.

MARIE *reaches to touch* JOAN*'s face.* DENNISON *looks uncomfortable.*

MARIE How do you get your skin so smooth?

DENNISON / Marie!

JOAN / Let's . . . uh . . . Let's make a toast!

MARIE Yes! Great idea. Dennison, pick up your glass!

JOAN Raymond.

RAYMOND *and* DENNISON *resentfully pick up their glasses.*

JOAN As I look around this table I see the past and I see the future.

I see four young people who are each changing the world around them in their own unique way: through the arts, law, sports, design, but all with passion and heart. Who have been fortunate to find each other and decided to embrace life and love.

At this table there is also a multitude of histories but with that comes the potential for a clean slate.

Conflict isn't always a bad thing; we all have beliefs and reasons for why we believe them. With conflict there is hope for change and growth; in our beliefs and in ourselves.

Nobody at this table is perfect. We all fight and argue. But, remember, it's so much easier to judge those who are closest to us because we know that their love is unconditional. We have love at this table in all different ways and forms. And that is invaluable.

Michelle Obama said, "You're not supposed to do this perfectly. You don't do life perfectly. No one does."

I say, what we can do perfectly is love each other's imperfections. So here is to our imperfections, to not doing life perfectly and to love.

To our first Christmas together and, most certainly, not our last.

EVERYONE Cheers!

They drink and start passing around food.

NARRATOR

Joan has written every speech that Ray ever spoke. No one knows this. Even Ray.

He thinks it is something they do together.

Joan always used to tell herself that Ray's work was for the greater good. That her work was his work, and his was hers. That as partners in life, they shared everything. His success was her success. But after all these years, Joan has started to question that dynamic.

The speech that went viral, the one for which Ray is being lauded around the nation, was Joan's finest work.

She wonders what would have happened if she had made that speech, if it was her in that video. If this Christmas it was her being talked about.

Everyone is eating, drinking and chattering. SONNY *places down his cutlery and clears his throat. He taps his champagne glass with his fork.*

SONNY I have an announcement.

MARIE Ooh, an announcement!

SONNY Christmas time is a time of gifts. It marks the birth of the world's greatest gift. A son. So, in saying this, I would like to announce that Rose and I / are—

JOAN Oh, my God! You're having a baby?!

ROSE What?

CHARLOTTE You're having a baby?!

JOAN / You're having a baby?!

RAY You're having a baby?!

SONNY We're having a baby?!

ROSE I'm having a baby?!

JOAN Sonny just said a gift /

SONNY / No, I was talking about Jesus. The Lord's son Jesus. He was our gift.

DENNISON/ RAY Here we go.

SONNY As we sit here we are celebrating the birth of Jesus, whether we think we are or not. We are here for Jesus. God gave up his son Jesus to save us. Think about that.

Now, as you already know, Rose and I are having our baptisms the first week after the New Year, and we would love to have your support and for you all to be there.

RAY You're getting baptised?

ROSE You would have received your invites over email.

RAY Why?

ROSE Because it's important to Sonn . . . It's important to us, Dad.

CHARLOTTE *speaks quietly to* ROSE.

CHARLOTTE I didn't think this was your / thing

ROSE / Not now, Char.

SONNY Dennison and Marie, we would love you to join us. But what I want you to all do, in the spirit of Christmas, is to close your eyes and let the Lord into your heart.

FRANCIS Wow . . . thank you for including us in your journey, Sonny . . . it's an honour . . .

SONNY No. Thank YOU, Francis.

Lord, I know it's hard to take steps. Sometimes we need to look to someone else to give us that push, Lord. And sometimes, you just need to dive in head first. Which is why I would like to tell you, Lord, that I am taking a year off JP Morgan Chase. Come March, Rose and I will be taking a year off to travel as missionaries and / serve—

ROSE Uh, what?

SONNY —our mission. To serve the Lord.

ROSE No, Sonny. Not this again. No.

JOAN You've only just come back.

RAY Great. We've got one daughter running around as a missionary and the other one moving to bloody New York /

CHARLOTTE / Dad!

JOAN Charlotte?!

ROSE Mum!?

RAY What?!

DENNISON His family is just like his politics: bloody chaos.

MARIE Dennison! Not now!

ROSE Sonny, I never agreed to this.

SONNY Rose, you agreed the day you let the Lord into your heart.

ROSE / I'm not going anywhere.

Sonny, we are not taking a year off. I have the Los Angeles store. You have a promotion coming up. No. Just . . . NO.

SONNY There is more than life to money and careers, Rose.

ROSE What about our plans for a family?

SONNY When the time is right. But now, now is the time to serve our family in here. *(taps his heart)*

DENNISON Doesn't he mean up there?

SONNY To serve the Lord.

ROSE We are not going to be fucking missionaries! I could do the baptisms. I could do the prayers. For God's sake, I could even do the speaking in tongues and exorcising the demons. But becoming missionaries? This phase is getting out of hand!

SONNY This isn't a phase!

ROSE It is a phase!

SONNY Rose, this is not a phase. It may be for you / but for me—

ROSE Okay, Sonny, my darling, "phase" may not have been the best word. But we need to think about this. We can't just pick up and go be missionaries.

SONNY But the Lord spoke to me, Rose. He spoke to me.

ROSE Can you all please excuse us? I think we need some air.

ROSE *drags* SONNY *out of the room.*

FRANCIS Well . . . that was intense.

JOAN They're going to be missionaries?! Can you believe that?

RAY When the Lord speaks, the Lord speaks.

JOAN The Lord? The boy clearly isn't dealing with the death of his father. Rose told me it was hard, but she didn't tell me it was this bad.

CHARLOTTE I kind of get what Sonny is saying.

FRANCIS What: about Jesus? You want us to convert?

CHARLOTTE About doing something bigger with your life. Something better.

FRANCIS For Jesus?

JOAN He's grieving and . . . looking for something . . . I don't know.

RAY He's not taking my daughter around the bloody world as a missionary. I don't care what's going on with him and I don't care if they want to do something bigger or better.

CHARLOTTE Because you know all about saving the world, Dad, and making it a better place.

DENNISON Well, he thinks he does.

MARIE For God's sake, Dennison, not now.

CHARLOTTE For himself, maybe.

RAY What is your problem, Charlotte?

CHARLOTTE We all have everything. Everything on the backs of others.

When do we have to give back a little?

Maybe that's what Sonny is saying.

FRANCIS That's very erudite, darling, but I think Sonny was talking very much about Jesus.

CHARLOTTE I don't know. Sonny works for JP Morgan Chase, for God's sake, maybe he just wants to try and make things right.

MARIE When have JP Morgan Chase ever hurt anyone?

JOAN *laughs.*

MARIE What? Why are you laughing?

JOAN That's a joke, right?

RAY Charlotte, we do not have everything on the "backs of other people".

CHARLOTTE You are so out of touch. It's ridiculous.

RAY What is going on, Char?

CHARLOTTE Look around, Dad!

RAY I'm looking, and what?

CHARLOTTE Look at everything we have!

RAY What I see are the fruits of hard work.

CHARLOTTE Don't pretend you don't know what I'm talking about.

RAY I don't know what you're talking about.

CHARLOTTE What about the law you made, that I used to win?

It was meant to help others and did the complete opposite!

RAY What others?

CHARLOTTE Stop being wilfully ignorant. The community. The Aboriginal community. How does this, all of this – everything we have – help them?

RAY This? This has nothing to do with them or those laws or helping . . . them.

CHARLOTTE This has everything to do with the / community—

RAY / Don't you dare judge my commitment to the community, Charlotte. When you say that you are not just judging me but where I come from. Where you come from.

CHARLOTTE Questioning and judging are different things.

RAY What happens under my roof is my business.

CHARLOTTE Oh, yes, your roof. Your huge property. Your Porsche and your Range Rover and your Mercedes. Your expensive suits and your speeches and your stupid VR headset. Look at you!

You've benefited pretty well from a community that has nothing to do with what goes on under your roof.

RAY Charlotte! How dare you talk to / me—

CHARLOTTE / You have so much.

RAY Well, I would say the same about you, Charlotte

CHARLOTTE Exactly. And that's why I don't want to take that stupid TV job. Because I don't want to do what you've done.

RAY What: you don't want a successful career!?

CHARLOTTE I'd rather have nothing than have everything if it costs other people.

Because that's what you did . . . we did.

RAY You'd rather have nothing? After everything I've given you.

CHARLOTTE / Yes, it's always about you. Your policies, your laws, your desire to lead, and your hope. That's your hope and and your hope only.

RAY My life has been about hope. My entire career.

CHARLOTTE That you built on the back of a community and have managed to create a fortune off.

RAY I worked hard.

CHARLOTTE The community hates you. They hate you.

JOAN Charlotte . . . that isn't true.

CHARLOTTE It is and you know it.

I bet you even wrote his speech, didn't you?

DENNISON I knew it!

MARIE Shut up, Dennison.

RAY I wrote that speech! Tell her, Joan.

JOAN I didn't . . . not . . . write it.

RAY She just helped.

JOAN Excuse me?

RAY I mean, she just helped me turn my thoughts into sentences—

JOAN Which is what writing is! Turning thoughts into sentences!

RAY I mean, you gave my thoughts words . . . and helped put those words into sentences.

JOAN That's writing, you fool!

FRANCIS That's true. Writing is just that.

RAY Those were my speeches! Your mother, she just . . . she . . .

JOAN She? I'm right here.

RAY You just helped!

JOAN I didn't just help! I don't want to be Black Hillary!

MARIE Oh, you're not Black Hillary.

DENNISON Who the fuck is Black Hillary?

RAY Are you happy now, Charlotte? Like a true teenager, having everyone fighting? Are you happy?

CHARLOTTE Am I happy? Of course I'm not happy.

RAY I gave you the best of everything. The best education, holidays, a roof over your heads, everything your mother and I never had. You're spoilt.

CHARLOTTE Yeah, I am.

Those communities we are celebrated for helping have nothing . . . absolutely nothing . . . because of the laws you made.

You fed me a lie. You said our successes are our communities' successes.

They're not. They're just ours. You did the wrong thing, Dad. So did I.

I'm ashamed to be your daughter.

RAY Get out.

CHARLOTTE *runs out of the room.* RAY *gets himself a drink.*

DENNISON I have an announcement to make myself.

If Christmas is as Sonny says it is, a time of giving, then unfortunately I am the Grinch.

MARIE Dennison, really? Now? You're timing has always been off. It's probably where Francis got it from.

FRANCIS How about I play some music? You know what they say . . . nothing.

MARIE Francis, timing, no.

DENNISON Now is the perfect time, Marie.

MARIE Dennison, they're clearly in the middle of something.

JOAN I hate to interrupt, Dennison, but maybe we should wait until after dessert when there have been more / drinks.

DENNISON / Well, with that—

MARIE Dennison, no.

DENNISON It's now or never, Marie. Francis, I have directed the lawyers to have you cut out of the trust.

FRANCIS What?

DENNISON I'm cutting you out of the trust.

FRANCIS It's a trust. You can't cut me off from the trust. Legally, you can't.

DENNISON No, I can. I had the lawyers look at it years ago.

FRANCIS Years? Oh, okay! You had the lawyers look at it years ago.

DENNISON You can't keep freeloading.

FRANCIS I'm not a freeloader, I'm a musician. A classical musician!

DENNISON Potato, potahto.

FRANCIS No one says "potahto", you idiot.

This is not your money to decide what to do with. That money comes from my grandparents.

DENNISON And they were my parents.

FRANCIS It's in a trust. A family trust that's there for all of us.

I rely on my allowance.

DENNISON And you need to learn to stand by your decisions and to be responsible. If you are responsible enough to get married, you're responsible enough to have your own financial income.

FRANCIS Yes! My trust!

DENNISON An income that you earn.

FRANCIS You didn't even know I was getting married.

DENNISON It's good timing then.

FRANCIS / So you're trying to blackmail me out of getting married?

DENNISON I'm actually trying to get you to invest in your life, Francis.

FRANCIS And what makes you think you have any right to do that?

DENNISON Because you don't support yourself!

FRANCIS And neither do you!

You have never had to.

Just because you got there first you think that gives you some kind of authority or moral high ground. You didn't work for a single thing and now you're condemning my freedom, the same freedom you had, because our values are different?

DENNISON If you can marry the daughter of my enemy, if you prance around Europe, you can look after yourself.

FRANCIS You hypocrite! You're a typical baby boomer.

DENNISON I am not a baby boomer.

FRANCIS Your parents supported you all the way through your career!

RAY I knew it!

JOAN Raymond, not now.

FRANCIS And you're going to leave me with nothing. You know, I knew you never wanted me. I knew it. But I thought at least some sense of guilt and propriety would mean you wouldn't touch what I'm entitled to. But no.

DENNISON You're not entitled to anything, Francis. That is your problem.

FRANCIS No, my problem is I don't have a family.

All my life I thought you were aware that you weren't very good parents.

That you knew you weren't great at letting me know you love me, or even being there for me.

I thought that by financially supporting me, you were at least making some gesture of care.

I'm an idiot, I thought the money was your love. I was wrong.

MARIE ... Francis, of course ... we do love you. Dennison?

DENNISON ...

MARIE Dennison, tell him.

DENNISON ...

FRANCIS You're a politician and you can't even lie to your own son.

We won't be able to go to New York. Charlotte and I, we won't have a future.

Mother?

MARIE I have no say, Francis. It's your father's family money.

FRANCIS *exits and stumbles into the kitchen, where* CHARLOTTE *has escaped to.*

CHARLOTTE Francis, are you okay?

FRANCIS Dennison ... he cut me out of the trust.

CHARLOTTE He cut you out of the trust? Can he even do that?

FRANCIS Yes.

What am I going to do? I have no money.

I'll have no career.

CHARLOTTE Why won't you have a career?

FRANCIS I won't be able to compose anymore.

I'll have to get a job.

I'm a mess. If you don't want to marry me, Charlotte. That's fine. That's totally fine.

I wouldn't want to marry me either. I understand.

You're not saying anything.

Oh, God.

You don't want to marry me, do you? Please don't not marry me. Please. I'll do anything /

CHARLOTTE / Francis, look at me.

FRANCIS / Oh, God, my life is ruined.

CHARLOTTE / Look at me.

CHARLOTTE *grabs* FRANCIS's *face and stares hard at it.*

CHARLOTTE I love you. I want to marry you.

FRANCIS Are you sure?

CHARLOTTE I'm sure.

FRANCIS I'm lucky you are so stupid.

CHARLOTTE I am very stupid. You are very lucky. Francis, it will be okay.

FRANCIS He couldn't even tell me he loves me, Charlotte.

CHARLOTTE I'm sorry, Francis.

FRANCIS This has really been the holiday from hell.

CHARLOTTE It's quite hilarious. I never would have thought it would go this badly.

FRANCIS I told you it would. I told you.

CHARLOTTE Your jokes didn't help.

FRANCIS Yes, sorry about that.

CHARLOTTE And the singing?

FRANCIS I told you I get awkward. Like actually awkward.

CHARLOTTE You were very awkward. I thought you meant, like, cute awkward but / no

FRANCIS / Yes, I know. Which is why I tried to tell you that, no, I get genuinely awkward. Terribly awkward. The kind of awkward where I make everyone in the room totally uncomfortable.

CHARLOTTE Sing it again.

FRANCIS Nope.

CHARLOTTE Please . . . pretty please.

FRANCIS "Ebony and ivory, live together in perfect harmony . . ."

CHARLOTTE "Isn't Francis so gifted?"

FRANCIS You do realise your dad doesn't even has his virtual reality mask turned on most of the time?

CHARLOTTE Don't even bring up my father. Sorry about my sister.

FRANCIS Sonny's a great guy, though. Aside from the Jesus stuff.

CHARLOTTE Well, you know: potato, potahto.

FRANCIS I don't think you know what that phrase means.

CHARLOTTE I don't. No idea.

Franny, you are good at lots of things. Not just the cello.

FRANCIS Would you like to name some of these things?

CHARLOTTE We'll move to New York and it'll just be me and you and Alicia Keys / in New York.

FRANCIS / About New York.

CHARLOTTE What about it?

FRANCIS Charlotte . . . Maybe your father is right. Maybe you should take the job.

CHARLOTTE My father?

FRANCIS He has a point about the TV job.

CHARLOTTE I can't take that job. I believe in what I said, Francis.

FRANCIS It will be great for your career.

CHARLOTTE You're scared.

FRANCIS I'm not scared, I just think you should think bigger picture. What is there for us in New York except for expensive rent and brownstones? You have so much here.

CHARLOTTE Don't pretend this is about me.

FRANCIS I'm being pragmatic. New York would be very hard now. Under our circumstances.

CHARLOTTE Our circumstances. So it's our circumstances now?

FRANCIS We are engaged, in case you've forgotten.

CHARLOTTE Oh, I haven't forgotten. Francis, you're acting like we're going to be living on rations.

FRANCIS I will have no money, Charlotte. None. I don't think you understand. My compositions don't exactly make it rain with cash money.

CHARLOTTE I'm a solicitor, Francis. I have savings and the scholarship and you'll get a job.

FRANCIS Or we won't go to New York and I will fight my father to get my share of the trust back!

CHARLOTTE / Your father is right. You are entitled!

You're afraid of having no money. You're afraid of working.

FRANCIS I am not afraid of working! Music is work.

CHARLOTTE You are being incredibly selfish.

FRANCIS Selfish?

CHARLOTTE You're all liberal and understanding until you actually have to give something up!

FRANCIS I am being understanding!

CHARLOTTE My father wants me to take a job because of his ego. His idea of legacy and his own relevance.

You want me to take the job because you can't stand the idea of being unsafe or having to take a risk.

FRANCIS That is not true!

CHARLOTTE It is totally true. You were all for New York when you could just fuck around and play the cello.

FRANCIS Oh, so I just fuck around / do I?

CHARLOTTE / Don't you dare turn this around!

FRANCIS Charlotte, you're angry with your father.

CHARLOTTE Don't patronise me.

I thought you weren't selfish and spoilt. That's what I loved about you: your humility. Your messy clothes and your vinegar smell.

But that's just a poor man's suit.

You live off an allowance and don't want to have to do anything on your own.

I don't want to be my mother.

I don't want to spend my life sacrificing what I want for love.

FRANCIS It's a TV job, Charlotte. Not a limb!

CHARLOTTE Is this what you really want: to stay in Australia?

To fight to not have a job?

Is that what you really want to do?

FRANCIS Yes.

CHARLOTTE Okay.

CHARLOTTE *takes off her ring and gives it back to* FRANCIS. CHARLOTTE *marches back to the dining room table. She sits down as everyone watches her. They eat and drink in silence.*

CHARLOTTE For God's sake, someone just ask instead of staring at me.

JOAN Well . . . what's going on?

CHARLOTTE / The engagement is off.

MARIE No!

DENNISON That was quick.

CHARLOTTE Yes, it is. And I bet you're all very happy.

RAY I knew it wasn't right. Right from the start. It's all timing. Martin Luther King had a saying about these kind of situations, "The time is always / right"—

JOAN / You're not Martin Luther King! For God's sake, not every Black man in Australia who puts two and two together and comes up with four is Martin Luther Fucking King!

You're just men, saying what us women have been saying for decades.

God, Ray, you think you're the only hope we have? After two daughters and a bypass, you're still thinking this is all about you? You fool! You selfish, selfish fool!

And now, you've single-handedly ruined your daughter's relationship!

RAY This isn't my fault!

JOAN Charlotte, is it?

CHARLOTTE It's at least half his fault.

JOAN See! It is your fault!

RAY It's not my fault, it's his fault!

RAY *points to* DENNISON.

DENNISON What?! This isn't my fault!

RAY It's always your fault!

DENNISON Why? Because I'm White!

RAY No! Because you're a . . . a cunt!

JOAN Raymond!

RAY And because you're White! That doesn't help either! It makes it worse!

DENNISON You're a racist!

RAY And you're a cunt!

JOAN Raymond, you take that back!

RAY No! He is!

MARIE He's kind of right.

DENNISON Marie!

RAY See! Even his own wife agrees. It's all his fault. If he had never had children this would never have happened! None of it!

DENNISON Well, maybe if you never had children this wouldn't have happened!

JOAN Both of you: stop it! Now!

MARIE You're as bad as each other!

ROSE *and* SONNY *come rushing in,* SONNY *holding up a bible.*

SONNY Everyone calm down! I have a bible! It's gonna be okay!

ROSE What is with all the yelling?

CHARLOTTE Francis and I have broken up. My life is ruined. Mum is blaming Dad and Dad is blaming Dennison.

ROSE Well . . . Good.

CHARLOTTE What do you mean, good?

ROSE It's probably for the best. You and Francis. You weren't meant to be together anyway. He's White and makes zero money.

JOAN Rose!

CHARLOTTE Rose, you're being a racist.

ROSE Umm . . . no, Charlotte. Everyone knows you can't be racist to a White person.

RAY This is true, my daughter.

CHARLOTTE Shut up, Dad!

ROSE Charlotte, did you know that 74 per cent of Aboriginal people get married to non-Aboriginal people? Did you know that?

CHARLOTTE What are you getting at?

ROSE We are a diminishing race. We need to procreate and make families and that's the key to empowerment.

Think of how races become successful: they stick together. They create communities. Economies. Like Beyoncé and Jay Z.

CHARLOTTE Beyoncé and Jay Z?

Rose, what the fuck are you talking about?

ROSE I'm talking about family! About making a strong Black community!

CHARLOTTE That sounds like racial propaganda.

ROSE I'm being pro-Black!

CHARLOTTE I love Francis!

ROSE Then just . . . un-love him.

CHARLOTTE You can't just tell me not to love him because he's White.

ROSE No, I'm telling you to be loyal to your community.

Our parents didn't fight for us to be successful so we would leave our culture behind and marry our oppressors.

CHARLOTTE We are the oppressors. We are the rich and powerful. We're not only NOT oppressed, we benefit from our political class. Surely someone else sees this.

ROSE Not being oppressed doesn't make us the oppressor.

We aren't White.

It's not potato potahto!

CHARLOTTE What does that saying even mean?

ROSE Don't marry a White man, Charlotte. Marry an Aboriginal. Like me.

CHARLOTTE Oh, my God, if you could only hear yourself right now. You sound like an idiot.

ROSE Stop calling me an idiot, Charlotte. I know you think I'm an idiot because I work in fashion. Because I didn't go to law school like you. Because I married a footballer—

SONNY Hey!

ROSE All of you think the same as Charlotte.

That because I'm not articulated or as educated or because I don't articulate good like the rest of you . . .

That doesn't mean I'm not intelligent and that I don't matter.

You dismiss me all so quickly. But I'm standing by what I just stood by and said.

I'm an educated businesswoman who runs an international clothing line. I will not be questioned for my decisions as a person who's questioned. I will not be dismissed.

I was raised to love being Black. Just like you were. And, yeah, I don't get on TV and sprout my opinion.

CHARLOTTE You're on TV all the time talking about fashion.

ROSE Don't say "fashion" like that. Like it's not important. Clothes are important! Because we wear them!

Just because I'm not doing PhDs in . . . racial identity politics /

CHARLOTTE / Post-colonial and cultural / studies—

ROSE / whatever the fuck you want to do a PDF in, but what I do and what I believe in matters as much as your wanker . . . stuff.

You're going on about us not doing anything for the Aboriginal community – at least I'm investing in it! Continuing it! I'm rich and Black, yeah! And I'm proud.

I'm going to have big Black babies. And they're going to know about their culture and their history because it's what both their parents are. You can all talk as much as you like, but what's the point of a thought if it stops with you?

And it's going to stop with you, Charlotte, if you don't stop fucking White men – like Francis.

I'm sorry, but it will.

CHARLOTTE You really think that?

ROSE Yes!

CHARLOTTE You stupid bitch.

CHARLOTTE *picks up a handful of food.* ROSE *picks up a handful of food too. They have a Mexican standoff.*

ROSE I know you are, but what am I?

CHARLOTTE A bitch.

ROSE Come on. Do it, Char. I dare you. This will be like Mother's Day 2006 all over again.

JOAN You promised no more fighting after that Mother's Day in 2006!

MARIE What happened on Mother's Day 2006?

SONNY We can't ever go back to Marigold Yum Cha again. None of us.

ROSE Do it, Charlotte! DO IT!

DENNISON How does it feel, Ray?

RAY What?

DENNISON To see everything you've created, your entire legacy, go up in smoke? Bit like your career, wouldn't you say? Or can't you answer without your wife?

ROSE Do it!

RAY *charges at* DENNISON. CHARLOTTE *pelts* ROSE *with food. A food fight erupts and* DENNISON *and* RAY *wrestle in the remains of lunch.* JOAN *is screaming at everyone to stop,* SONNY *is praying and* MARIE *calmly tops up her champagne and basks in the chaos.*

JOAN Watch the crystal!

NARRATOR

The word "family" is derived from the Latin term *familia*. It is a group of people affiliated by birth or by affinity and shared kinship.

That's all.

This lot don't know it yet, and they might not look it . . .

But they are a family.

A phone starts ringing. Amid the chaos, SONNY *starts searching for it. He finally finds it and answers.*

SONNY Hi.

Yeah, good thanks.

Sorry . . . I can't hear you.

I can't hear you, you'll have to speak up!

You have the results?

Sorry?

I'm what?!

What?!

I'M NOT ABORIGINAL?!

SONNY*'s revelation silences the room. Everyone stops and looks at him. He hangs up the phone.*

SONNY I'm not Aboriginal . . . The show. They said my DNA results show that I'm . . . I'm

Tongan?

I'm Tongan.

ROSE How?

SONNY My dad . . . isn't Aboriginal . . .

ROSE You mean your mum isn't Aboriginal?

SONNY They're telling me Dad wasn't either.

ROSE Sonny, you can't be Tongan.

SONNY Rose, I'm Tongan.

ROSE You were the Aboriginal captain of the Wallabies, for God's sake! Aboriginal!

We are meant to be the Aboriginal Kim and Kanye. Beyoncé and Jay Z.

When this goes to air . . .

Oh, shit. This will be on TV.

People are going to see this.

Everyone's going to know.

SONNY Rose, darling, God has a plan /

ROSE / Fuck God's plan! What about my plan!? What about our family?! What about our beautiful, Black babies?

ROSE *storms out.* SONNY *goes to follow.*

JOAN It's probably best you don't.

JOAN *follows* ROSE *out.*

RAY Come on, Sonny. Let's get some air.

RAY *leads* SONNY *out.* CHARLOTTE *is left standing with the* SMITHS. *There is an awkward silence.*

CHARLOTTE Well . . . thank you so much for coming to my family's holiday home this festive season . . . Marie and Dennison.

MARIE Thank you so much for having us.

CHARLOTTE It's been a very . . . full time so far. I should let you have some time . . . to yourselves . . . to be . . . by yourselves. Goodbye.

CHARLOTTE *makes a swift yet awkward exit.*

DENNISON Bloody family time? I need to get some air from this bloody humpee. I'm going to go sit in the car. Where are the keys? Marie, where'd I put the keys? Marie?

MARIE I'm sure you'll figure it out, Dennison.

DENNISON *mumbles on the way out.* MARIE *sits with a drink by herself for a few moments. She seems very calm. She checks her phone. After a while,* FRANCIS *walks in. He pours himself a drink and sits down next to his mum.*

FRANCIS What's going on here?

MARIE Well . . . I . . . I don't even know.

Sonny's Tongan.

FRANCIS Sonny? He's not Aboriginal?

MARIE I guess not. To be honest, he does look Tongan. I don't understand how nobody realised.

FRANCIS Mum, I saw you on Tinder when we were in London.

MARIE Play something for me. You always played so beautifully.

FRANCIS Mum.

MARIE Please?

FRANCIS Why does Dad hate me?

MARIE He doesn't hate you.

FRANCIS He doesn't love me.

MARIE He does.

FRANCIS He couldn't say it.

MARIE He doesn't know how to.

Trust me, I know.

FRANCIS He has made a pretty clear decision.

MARIE It was an empty threat.

FRANCIS He hasn't cancelled my trust?

MARIE No.

FRANCIS Then why did he say all that?

MARIE He hasn't, but that doesn't mean that he won't.

But really, Francis, you shouldn't live on your trust.

FRANCIS What do you mean?

MARIE I think you should take your father's threat as advice.

You should find some financial independence.

FRANCIS I don't think you understand how hard that / is.

MARIE / You don't think I understand how hard it is? I completely understand how hard it is to not have money.

But you can't base your decisions on what is easy, Francis.

FRANCIS You're staying with Dad for the money, aren't you?

MARIE And, unfortunately now, because I'm rather fond of him. Your father and I have both made decisions based around money. Mine, my marriage. Your father, his career, and with that came the sacrifice of many things: love, empathy, kindness.

FRANCIS But when you say that, you say it like there was never any of that in your life. Like we were never a family, like you never loved Dad or me.

MARIE Not at all. I love you very much. But if I had been braver earlier in my life, it may have been different. I was scared.

I never lived the life I wanted because if I left Dennison, I would have nothing. So I stayed.

And now . . . now I don't know what life could have been like if I had been brave.

Francis, don't make the mistake I did.

FRANCIS *gives his mother a kiss. He goes back to playing the cello.* JOAN *walks in. She sits and listens with* MARIE. FRANCIS *eventually stops and lays down his bow.*

JOAN You play beautifully, Francis.

FRANCIS Thank you.

MARIE Francis, give us a moment.

FRANCIS *leaves.* JOAN *gets out a cigarette and opens a window. She starts to smoke.*

JOAN Despite all this, it's been nice seeing you again, Marie.

MARIE I like you.

JOAN I know.

But.

Well, what can I say?

MARIE Not much.

JOAN I'm flattered.

MARIE Have you ever thought what life would have been like if you made the opposite decision to every one you've ever made?

JOAN Yes, I have.

MARIE Are you happy?

JOAN As much as anyone could be.

Are you?

MARIE As much as I ever will be.

How did we end up with these awful men?

JOAN Ray wasn't always awful. He isn't most of the time.

Most of the time he's just Ray.

That's why I'll always love him.

MARIE Can I kiss you?

JOAN Go on, then.

JOAN *and* MARIE *start to kiss.* DENNISON *walks in.*

DENNISON What the fuck?

RAY *walks into the room with the virtual reality headset on his head, just as* JOAN *and* MARIE *break apart.*

DENNISON Oh, my fucking God!

RAY What's going on? *(takes off his headset)* Oh.

JOAN I can explain!

MARIE It's exactly what it looked like, Dennison.

RAY A bit late in the game for this, isn't it, Joan?

DENNISON Oh, my God.
The list was right!

MARIE What?

DENNISON You're cheating on me!
I knew it!
I googled "How to know if your partner is cheating on you" and this list came up.

A list with the top seven signs. I read them and you did every one. You were on your phone all the time, you were always changing your passwords on the computer, you started dressing / nicer—

MARIE / For God's sake, Dennison!

DENNISON You were cheating on me!
All this time!
With Joan!

JOAN What?

MARIE Yes, Dennison, I'm cheating on you.
But not with Joan.
With lots of people.

JOAN Excuse me, I'm going to wash my mouth now.

DENNISON You're staying here!
You're all staying here.
What do you mean, lots of people?

MARIE I have been very unhappy and unfulfilled for many years, Dennison.

After immense googling and research, I have come to the realisation that I am Queer.

DENNISON You're a gay?

MARIE No, I'm Queer. It's different.

DENNISON How?

MARIE It's less binary.

DENNISON What do you mean, less binary?

MARIE Queer doesn't make assumptions about who you are or who you love.

I'm polyamorous, and I identify as Queer.

DENNISON When did you plan to tell me this?

MARIE I was going to wait till New Year, but it's better you find out now.

DENNISON You've broken my heart.

MARIE No, I haven't.

DENNISON Yes, you have!

MARIE No, I haven't.

DENNISON Yes, you have!

MARIE You don't have a heart.

DENNISON I did, and you broke it!

I love you!

We're bonded by the sanctimonious ties of marriage!

MARIE You only married me because you had to, Dennison. Because it was easy.

DENNISON Marriage with you was not easy.

MARIE Don't give me that shit.

DENNISON Well, it isn't now!

Are you sleeping with people too?

Are you?

MARIE It depends what you mean by "sleeping".

DENNISON Sleeping! Slept! Had intercourse! Sex! Have you?

MARIE I haven't had penetrative sex with anyone yet.

But I've made love other ways. Yes.

Really, why is it such a surprise to you? You haven't touched me in years.

DENNISON You haven't touched me!

RAY Penetrative sex?

JOAN You know . . . In the, you know . . .

RAY Oh.

DENNISON All these years to just get a divorce.

MARIE We don't have to divorce.

I had no plan to divorce you after I came out.

We'll just stay together like we always have.

And we can just see other people.

DENNISON See other people? Like sluts? Great, we'll be a pair of old sluts. Just slutting around together.

MARIE This is not a joke, Dennison. I'm not a joke.

You deserve the truth and I deserve a shot at having a life.

At feeling lust and being lusted over.

We deserve to live, Dennison. And even if you don't choose to, I want to.

I want to know who I am and what I like and what feels good. I want to know myself.

DENNISON It's Christmas, Marie! It's Christmas!

And I catch you making out with Ray Gibson's wife?

Well, guess what, Marie! I can kiss lots of people too!

See how you like it now, Marie!

DENNISON *tries to kiss* JOAN, *but is slow in his tears.*

JOAN Dennison – please.

RAY Come on, mate. Come on.

DENNISON I can live and try stuff too!

As RAY *pulls* DENNISON *away,* DENNISON *tries to kiss* RAY.

RAY Hey! Look out! Stop that!

RAY *pushes him away and* DENNISON *falls to the floor, sobbing.*

JOAN — You take care of that.

How about we go find the children?

MARIE — Get it together, Dennison.

I gave you everything you ever wanted. I gave you a life. Don't make me feel bad for wanting one of my own. And for chrissakes, it's Ma*rie*.

JOAN *and* MARIE *leave.*

RAY — Come on, mate. Really, don't cry. You'll be fine.

In fact, a lot of men wish they were in your position.

DENNISON — I love her. I do.

RAY — I'm sure you do.

DENNISON — Everyone hates me.

RAY — No, they don't.

DENNISON — Yes, they do. My son hates me, my wife hates me.

RAY They don't hate you. That's how families act. We all do. Being selfish with how we think everyone should behave. You should be used to it by now, Dennison. We were politicians.

DENNISON You hate me.

RAY Dennison . . . Dennison . . . I don't hate you.

DENNISON You're lying.

RAY I'm not lying.

DENNISON You don't hate me?

RAY I don't.

DENNISON You really mean that?

RAY . . . Yeah. I guess.

DENNISON It's not that she's Queer.

It's just . . . nobody telling me anything. That I'm not part of their lives. That's what hurts.

Because I know it's my fault.

RAY You think you're doing the right thing and then it turns out you have no idea what the right thing is.

DENNISON Did you ever think this is where we would end up?

RAY No. Not quite.

DENNISON Two old men with no relevance who don't even understand their own families.

RAY Well, when you put it like that.

But I didn't think I'd have a virtual reality headset either. So you win some, you lose some.

DENNISON What if we lose Francis and Charlotte?

Maybe I never even had Francis to begin with.

RAY I wasn't the best father.

DENNISON Me neither.

RAY That's what I was getting at.

Dennison, if you love your son, you need to let him know.

DENNISON I don't know how.

RAY You say it.

DENNISON Maybe we can make things better, get the kids back together.

What about some kind of agreement . . . between us . . . over them.

RAY Like a . . . like a treaty?

DENNISON Like a treaty!

How about we make a treaty!

RAY . . . That's not a half bad idea.

DENNISON Bet you never thought you'd hear that word coming out of my mouth. Treaty.

Treaty. Treaty.

RAY I sure didn't.

DENNISON Where do we start?

RAY So: "We, Ray Gibson and Dennison Smith, the fathers of the respective parties, hereby give our permission . . . blah . . . blah . . . "

DENNISON This remind you of something?

RAY Of the good old days?

DENNISON It does, doesn't it? Making laws, disagreeing. Agreeing.

RAY Making change.

DENNISON Feels good.

RAY I'll go get my iPad and we can write it up.

RAY *and* DENNISON *shake hands.* RAY *exits.* CHARLOTTE *enters with some cake.* DENNISON *and* CHARLOTTE *look at each other. He pats the ground next to him.* CHARLOTTE *sits with* DENNISON *and they share cake and drink scotch.*

DENNISON He had great hair, your father. A whole head of it.

CHARLOTTE A whole head of hair and a whole lot of lies.

DENNISON Don't be so hard on your father.

Do you love my son? Really love him?

CHARLOTTE Yes.

DENNISON Then why end it?

CHARLOTTE I thought he stood for more.

DENNISON He brought me here to your father's house. He stands for things.

CHARLOTTE He tried to get out of it.

DENNISON Of course he did. He's not an idiot. Look at us.

CHARLOTTE He just expected me to drop our dream in an instant.

DENNISON You know Francis isn't a naturally gifted cellist?

CHARLOTTE What are you talking about? He's brilliant!

DENNISON But he's not naturally gifted. He technically doesn't have the right hands.

He worked hard. He practised every day as a child for hours on end.

Francis is not afraid of hard work.

Francis is afraid of becoming like me.

DENNISON *and* CHARLOTTE *finish the cake.* SONNY *enters the room.*

SONNY Have you seen my bible?

CHARLOTTE, DENNISON *and* SONNY *search the room for the bible, tearing it apart.* CHARLOTTE *leaves.*

DENNISON Found it, mate.

DENNISON *hands* SONNY *the bible.* SONNY *sits with the bible and a drink. He opens it up and pulls out a picture of his dad.*

DENNISON Is that your father?

FRANCIS *walks in, playing his instrument.*

FRANCIS Am I disturbing anything?

SONNY No, not really.
Hey – can you play anything by Tupac?

FRANCIS Not really.

SONNY Okay.

FRANCIS I can play "You're the Voice" by John Farnham.

SONNY I'll be fine.

SONNY Everyone just said I had a touch of Chinaman or something far back.

I wonder if my dad knew? I don't know which is worse: that he didn't know he wasn't Aboriginal, or if he knew he was Tongan and lied? Lied to me my entire life?

FRANCIS What's your favourite memory of your dad?

SONNY When he used to take me fishing. After church every Sunday. We'd go down to the river, just him and I, and talk for hours. Then we'd come home and cook up the fish for the mob.

FRANCIS Then does it matter if he knew or didn't know? Nothing changes who your dad was, how he loved you and your family and your community.

RAY *enters; he has been listening the entire time.*

RAY So I have one Tongan and one White son.

SONNY Did you ever suspect?

RAY Honestly? Thought you might have had a touch of something.

SONNY If this changes anything /

RAY / Sonny. It's right. You're still part of the family. You're still Sonny. Just give the Jesus stuff a break.

SONNY Ray, I had an Aboriginal scholarship through school and uni.

I was Aboriginal captain of the Wallabies.

I was the Aboriginal sportsman of the year. I'm the ambassador for the Aboriginal kids sports fund.

My idea of who I am was based on this one thing.

And it was never true.

I'm a fraud.

RAY You didn't know.

SONNY I made money off being Aboriginal, Ray.

RAY Do you want to know why Charlotte is so mad at me?

Back when I was in politics, I helped get through laws that would allow Aboriginal people to negotiate land leases with corporations who wanted to use their land.

I wanted to win so badly that I agreed to what has turned out to be a very awful clause. Just to get the laws through. Just to win.

That clause has been very disadvantageous to many Aboriginal people.

All because of my ambition.

I fought other battles. Thought I could make up for it. I never had to face the community. Was never confronted with the reality of what I'd done. Until Charlotte found out.

Something happened to me as I got older. I stopped questioning the ground I stood on. You start to think it's all about you. You start to think hope isn't a real thing.

You need to be there for your community, Sonny.

That's what Rose cares about.

SONNY Thanks, Ray.

SONNY *exits.*

RAY That was very decent of you, Francis. What you said to Sonny.

FRANCIS You said a Tongan son and a White son.

RAY . . . Well, I thought, shit, if you can love my daughter and make her happy, I have to love you too.

FRANCIS I love you too, Dad.

RAY Too soon, Francis.

You're on probation.

Six months probation for nudity.

And six months for not asking me first for permission to marry my daughter.

FRANCIS I didn't ask your permission because as a feminist / I believe a woman has a right—

RAY / Okay, okay. As a fellow feminist, good answer. Six months only then, Francis.

If Charlotte loves you, she'll do anything for you. Just like her mother.

Don't make the same mistake I did. Don't make everything about you. Don't make her sacrifice her dreams.

FRANCIS I want to fight for her.

New York, Alicia Keys, / Brownstones—

RAY / Alicia Keys?

Do you love my daughter, Francis?

FRANCIS Of course, I do!

RAY Then let's go and get her back! Ready?!

FRANCIS Ready!

RAY I can't hear you! READY?!

FRANCIS READY!

RAY *and* FRANCIS *leave.* CHARLOTTE *and* ROSE *enter. They start tidying up.*

NARRATOR

Each of these people has a secret: about who they are or what they've done or who they want to be. Joan is very lonely sometimes.

Ray went to a consultation for hair plugs, but he is worried he left it too late.

Rose is scared she will be a terrible mother.

Charlotte once had a crush on Fatty Vautin.

Francis once applied for business school but was rejected.

Sonny cheated on an online test to become a marriage celebrant.

Dennison has been learning to play the banjo and Marie wonders if something is wrong with her because she has never had a hobby.

At the end of the day, they are all people and they are all scared and they are all trying to get by and love.

CHARLOTTE Do you really think all those things? About races sticking together to survive?

ROSE I don't know. I've had these views my entire life, Charlotte.

CHARLOTTE But what about Sonny?

ROSE I didn't mean what I said, Char. I'm not going to love you or your children any less.

Although I could do without Dennison Smith in my life.

CHARLOTTE It's not just my kids, but their kids and their kids. Would you call them Black?

Would you call them family?

JOAN *appears. She squeezes down in the middle of them with champagne and glasses.*

JOAN — I'm glad to see you both talking. I feel like I should flog you both over the food fight.

JOAN *starts pouring the champagne and handing out glasses.*

CHARLOTTE — Mum, what if your grandchildren are White? How would you feel?

JOAN — They'll be Aboriginal. Because you are.

NARRATOR — *"Mmhmm . . ."*

CHARLOTTE — That's not what Rose said before.

ROSE — I don't know, Charlotte. It's confusing.

JOAN — Both of you, stop getting so caught up on Black and White. Race is values, the same as any other construct in life. But values aren't people. If you forget about people, your victories can turn into your vices in a heartbeat.

If this isn't the life you want, give it up. You can blame your father for what he has done in the past, but don't blame him for your future. We didn't raise you like that.

Live what you believe in. Keep questioning your privilege and those who have power.

Both of you have self-determination. I've made sure of that. So use it.

JOAN *pulls a joint out of her bra. She lights it and takes a toke and offers it to the girls. She falls into the couch.*

JOAN Now, after this one, no more. I want grandkids.

MARIE *enters.*

MARIE Do I smell marijuana?

JOAN *passes* MARIE *the joint.*

JOAN Here.

MARIE Goodie.

This is good shit.

JOAN It's from David Joneses.

ROSE Sonny's Tongan. Sonny is Tongan. Sonny is Tongan. I've never said that out loud before.

MARIE You better get used to it.

FRANCIS *starts playing "Mysterious Girl" as* SONNY, RAY *and* DENNISON *carry him in.*

CHARLOTTE Don't say anything.

FRANCIS *stops and gets down on one knee.* CHARLOTTE *steps forward to* FRANCIS *and pulls him up.*

CHARLOTTE You were wrong before. And being spoilt. And truth be told, sometimes you still smell slightly of vinegar but I love you, Francis Smith. And I was wrong too. Sometimes I say things like "artisanal bread shop" and maybe I do romanticise the working class.

It scared me that you gave up on our dream so quickly, but I realise that what I wanted was for you to give up everything to follow my dream. That's not fair.

FRANCIS I was scared. And I was wrong. I gave up quickly, but that's not who I am, Charlotte.

I fight for what I love and I promise to never give up on you or us again.

CHARLOTTE Let's go to New York.

FRANCIS *hands* CHARLOTTE *a piece of paper.*

FRANCIS I already booked the tickets.

CHARLOTTE *gets down on one knee.*

CHARLOTTE Francis Smith . . . will you marry me?

FRANCIS Yes.

CHARLOTTE *hands* FRANCIS *a ring box.*

CHARLOTTE Don't open it. It's empty. I just thought it would add to the drama.

CHARLOTTE *and* FRANCIS *kiss.*

RAY Dennison and I have an agreement we have signed.

DENNISON About our behaviour and how to share time.

RAY It's called the Ebony . . .

DENNISON . . . and Ivory Treaty of 2017.

CHARLOTTE Are you serious?

DENNISON We've both signed and stamped it.

FRANCIS *reads it. He starts to laugh.*

CHARLOTTE Let me see that.

CHARLOTTE *starts to laugh as well.*

RAY We've agreed to not be dickheads and to keep our opinions to ourselves.

DENNISON Except when asked. And even then, we'll consult before sharing.

CHARLOTTE Dad.

FRANCIS Thank you, Dad.

DENNISON Francis, I love you.

FRANCIS I love you too, Dad.

CHARLOTTE *hugs both* RAY *and* DENNISON.

SONNY Rose, I'm sorry. I'm sorry I'm not Aboriginal or the man you fell in love with. Do you forgive me?

ROSE Of course I don't forgive you. You have nothing to be sorry about.

Sonny, you will always be the man I fell in love with.

SONNY Always . . .

Unless a ghost or non-human entity took possession of me. Or I had a brain replacement and then I would be somebody else in my body.

ROSE Yep!

SONNY I don't know if God has a plan. I just miss my dad, Rose.

ROSE I know.

DENNISON Marie, I have something to say to you.

MARIE Yes, Dennison?

DENNISON I accept you and your sexual identity and . . . your polyamory. I just hope that next time you are seeking sexual pleasure, you consider myself to join you before your other suitors . . . if that's okay?

MARIE Dennison, it's been twelve years since you last kissed me with tongue!

DENNISON I . . . Look, it's been . . . after a certain age . . .

MARIE Fuck it. Kiss me, Dennison.

MARIE *and* DENNISON *kiss with tongue.*

RAY Joan, I'm thinking about quitting Twitter.

JOAN . . . That's it?

RAY What?

JOAN All of this honesty and romance and you just tell me you're quitting goddam Twitter?

RAY For you, Joan! For you! Because I love you, I'm quitting Twitter!

JOAN Come here, you big oaf.

FRANCIS We're going to New York!

CHARLOTTE And getting married!

FRANCIS Just in case you'd forgotten.

SONNY Why wait? I would like to do one thing for you.

ROSE Sonny is a celebrant!

SONNY I got a certificate on the internet. Let me marry you.

CHARLOTTE Yes.

FRANCIS It'd be our honour.

FRANCIS *and* CHARLOTTE *stand before* SONNY.

SONNY Ready?

FRANCIS/
CHARLOTTE Ready.

SONNY Look, I don't really remember anything from the course. I skipped a lot.

Anyways, I now pronounce you, husband and wife.

MYSTERIOUS GIRL *starts to play. They dance. Everyone dances. It's a happy ending.*

NARRATOR

They were a tribe.
A lost tribe.

An old tribe.
A new tribe.
And no matter where they end up or who they become, they will all live happily ever after.
Because they are all very rich.
The end.

THE END.

ORIGINAL CAST AND CREW

Black is the New White was first produced by Sydney Theatre Company at Wharf 1 Theatre on 10 May 2017 with the following cast and creative team:

Francis Smith
James Bell

Rose Jones
Kylie Bracknell (Kaarljilba Kaardn)

Ray Gibson
Tony Briggs

Narrator
Luke Carroll

Marie Smith
Vanessa Downing

Dennison Smith
Geoff Morrell

Joan Gibson

Melodie Reynolds-Diarra

Charlotte Gibson

Shari Sebbens

Sonny Jones

Anthony Taufa

Director

Paige Rattray

Designer

Renée Mulder

Lighting Designer

Ben Hughes

Composer & Sound Designer

Steve Toulmin

Assistant Director

Julia Patey

Voice & Text Coach

Charmian Gradwell

Production Manager

Whitney Eglington

Stage Manager

Todd Eichorn

ABOUT THE AUTHOR

Nakkiah Lui is a co-writer and star of *Black Comedy* and co-host of the Buzzfeed podcast *Pretty for an Aboriginal.* She has been a playwright-in-residence for Sydney's Belvoir Theatre and artist-in-residence for the Griffin Theatre. Most recently Nakkiah has appeared as a regular guest on *Screen Time* on ABC and her new six-part comedy series, *Kiki & Kitty*, premiered on ABC in 2017. She is a Gamilaroi/Torres Strait Islander woman and a leader in the Australian Aboriginal community.